T0308631

NUMEROLOGY

UPDATED SIXTH EDITION

ROSEMAREE TEMPLETON

NUMEROLOGY

UPDATED SIXTH EDITION

ROCKPOOL
PUBLISHING

THIS BOOK IS DEDICATED
TO THE MEMORY OF MY GRANDMOTHER
HETTIE TEMPLETON
AND TO MY FAMILY

A Rockpool book
PO Box 252, Summer Hill, NSW 2130, Australia
www.rockpoolpublishing.com.au
http://www.facebook.com/RockpoolPublishing

First published in 2008
Copyright © RoseMaree Templeton 2008
This edition published in 2016

All rights reserved. No part of this publication may be reproduced,
stored in a retrieval system, or transmitted in any form or by any means,
electronic, mechanical, photocopying, recording or otherwise, without
the prior written permission of the publisher.

National Library of Australia Cataloguing-in-Publication entry

Templeton, RoseMaree, author.
Numerology / RoseMaree Templeton.
Updated 6th edition.

ISBN: 9781925429022 (hardback)

Numerology.

133.335

Cover by Zvaigzne ABC (Latvia)
Edited by Desney Shoemark
Editorial assistance by Katie Evans
Typeset by Typeskill
Printed and bound in China
10 9 8 7 6 5 4 3 2

All rights reserved. No part of this publication may be reproduced,
stored in a retrieval system, or transmitted in any form or by any means,
electronic, mechanical, photocopying, recording or otherwise,
without the prior written permission of the publisher.

CONTENTS

PREFACE

This book is based on the work of my grandmother Hettie Templeton (1887–1967) who was one of the first Australian numerologists and the first president of the Pythagorean Society in Australia. Her studies in this field began long before 1940 when she devised a simple four-line chart for birthdate numbers. Noticing that the charts had certain patterns, which she named 'arrows', she developed from this insight a line of research based on the work of Pythagoras, the ancient Greek mathematician and philosopher. As her knowledge and experience grew, Hettie became much sought after as an adviser and teacher. During the 1940s and 1950s she was the foremost numerologist in Australia, presenting her own talk-back radio program in Sydney.

Using her own methods, Hettie Templeton worked for years among children and adults, accumulating enough evidence to prove that numerology held some real value. In 1940 she published *Numbers and their Influence*, which she updated in 1956 with *A Philosophy of Numbers*. She

Hettie Templeton (1887–1967) was Australia's foremost numerologist during the early and mid 20th century

realised her methods were unorthodox, but wrote and taught in the certainty that her knowledge could help parents to better understand their children. It was important, she wrote, for parents to know the inner natures of their children and to understand the reasons for the differences between them. Her claim was that a correct understanding of the law of numbers would reveal the general characteristics of any person.

Hettie Templeton's writing and my personal notes taken from her lectures provide the foundation of my thinking on this subject. This book explains how the power of numerology can help people cope with everyday problems and challenges of living. My contribution has been to rewrite and expand Hettie Templeton's work, making it more accessible and relevant for modern readers. Templeton's knowledge of numerology, as reinterpreted and expanded here, is a treasury of good advice for people of all ages, although her greatest wish was that it be used to help children.

All readers who study and utilise the wisdom and insights revealed here through numerology are likely to gain useful understanding of their own nature, their personal attributes and characteristics, and ways in which to apply this awareness in daily life.

INTRODUCTION

In sixth century Egypt, the priests of Memphis taught:
'The science of numbers and the art of the will are the two
keys of magic. They open all the doors of the universe.'

THE GREAT INITIATES, EDOUARD SCHURE

MANY BOOKS have been published about numerology since Hettie Templeton published *Numbers and their Influence* in 1940. Some writers have over-complicated the subject, and there is need for a return to the basics of self-help numerology, expressed in a form that is easy to read and understand. For anyone embarking on these studies, it is useful to have an overview of the Pythagorean foundations of Hettie's work. She described it this way: 'Pythagoras, the Greek philosopher ... born about 580 BC, is known as the first Master who understood Numbers ... His teaching was that Number [is] the first principle of the universe, and on it depends the harmonies which keep the universe in ordered notation ...'

Each person is born with certain abilities, talents and tendencies, and their personal numbers (those associated with their birthdate and their name) reveal the details.

People who understand the vibrational power of numbers will also understand their own strengths and weaknesses, and those of others, and how best to take advantage of circumstances, favourable and unfavourable, that will occur during their lives. In 1940, Hettie Templeton wrote: 'All is vibration, proportion, number, and we are ruled, influenced and impressed by such. It is now generally realised that everything is vibration, which is the life behind all things. Number ... is a living force; it is proportion, or form. It is the vibration of life in its various dimensions, that creates all forms manifesting life ... It is the underlying basis of order and rhythm.'

Understanding is achieved by reading a chart drawn up from an individual's birthdate in conjunction with their ruling number, day number, personal year number, name chart and pyramid chart, all of which are introduced and explained in this book.

Each decade and each century, because of the commonality of their defining numbers, has certain signature characteristics. For example, children born between the years 2000 and 2009 inclusive will have fewer numbers than usual in their birthdates, resulting in an increased chance that up to eight squares in their charts will be empty of numbers. As revealed in the chapters that follow, such events can have certain negative or challenging consequences. The 'empty' arrows highlight specific life lessons the individual is likely to confront. In these circumstances, as well as with other personal weaknesses revealed in charts, parents will find that the power of numerology will better equip them to take compensatory remedial action.

People of all ages and at any stage in their life will find the information in this book valuable because it helps reveal the life path of a soul from the cradle to mature adulthood. All those who want to know what makes themselves and others tick will benefit; application of the awareness gained will assist in minimising conflict within families, groups and communities.

HOW TO USE THIS BOOK

To gain the most from this book and develop a balanced understanding of numerology, readers must be aware of two important points.

First, numbers are important indicators of a person's strengths and weaknesses *but they need not dictate the events of that person's life*. For example, people having three 2s in their birthdate are often absorbed in a world of their own and are sometimes known as dreamers. They are hypersensitive, particularly as children, and are quick to imitate. This does not mean that absolutely everyone with three 2s will be dreamers and hypersensitive, but it does mean that there will be a strong tendency for them to be that way.

Second, *no single element or aspect of numerology should be interpreted as a comprehensive statement about a person's strengths and weaknesses.* A complete picture will be gained only after taking into account the influence of every element, that is, after examining the whole of the birthdate chart, the arrows, the ruling number, the day number, the personal year number, the name numbers and the pyramids (if applicable). For example, the tendencies mentioned above — of a person with three 2s in their birthdate chart — might be somewhat counterbalanced should that same person have all three numbers (1, 4, 7) on the earth plane of the chart. An example birthdate is 27/12/2004.

Birthdate

222		
1	**4**	**7**

For this individual, the absence of numbers on the mind plane — 3, 6, 9 — will accentuate the possibility of them being considered a 'dreamer', so the practicality reinforced by the 1, 4, 7 is especially valuable.

If you want to dabble in sections of the book, this summary of the following chapters will help.

• For an in-depth general understanding of each of the numbers, see Chapter 1.

- If you want to have a look at your birthdate chart to see where your numbers are placed and what they mean, go to page 101 and follow the easy method.
- If you just want to know your ruling number, add all the digits of your birthdate. The sum is your ruling number. See page 14.
  Ruling numbers are: 2, 3, 4, 5, 6, 7, 8, 9, 10, 11, 22/4. So whatever the total of your birthdate numbers, it must be reduced to one of the above numbers: for example, 21=3; 25=7; 37=10; etcetera. Note that 22/4 is not reduced.
- If you would like to see which arrows you have on your chart, go to Chapter 4.
- The arrows give added information and also tell you where your strengths and weaknesses lie.

Perhaps you want to know your influences for the current year. This is always relevant when considering major life decisions. Maybe you want to buy or sell property. Perhaps meet someone new? Perhaps go on a trip? Maybe do some study?

- Add the numbers of the day of birth, the month of birth and the current year together. The resulting number is called the personal year number (PYN). See page 86.
- To see 'the other side of you', go to page 79 and read about your day number.
- Want to check out your name on a chart and compare it with your birthdate chart? Go to page 151.

We change, learn and grow through various cycles and stages in our lives. Understanding what these phases are and how to map them can be most helpful. To see where you're up to, you'll want to look at your pyramids.

Follow the method carefully and you'll soon get the hang of it. See page 180.

Once you have dabbled, you will probably be so fascinated that you will want to come back to the beginning and make a more comprehensive study of numerology's complexities and the insights they reveal.

Chapter 1

THE SYMBOLISM
OF NUMBERS

In a mysterious way, the understanding of numbers enables us at once to know the character and general tendencies of each life event, whether universal or of the individual. Number is the basis of all created life, and unless and until man knows and understands numbers, he cannot fully understand life and its expressions. By the aid of this understanding of the Science of Numbers, man can see far beyond the normal outlook, far beyond the outer man or event, to the soul of things.

NUMBERS AND THEIR INFLUENCE, HETTIE TEMPLETON

When we first hear of numbers influencing human nature in any way, many of us are likely to question how this could possibly be.

The origin of numbers is uncertain and ancient. Although the numbers we use today have changed in design, numbers have been in use for at least 5500 years. The Arabs, who might have borrowed them from the Hindus, employed them — and if we consult these people we are told that numbers come from the gods.

Pythagoras, the first person to claim and offer a universal understanding on the subject, has become known as the father of number analysis. He was convinced that the universe, including and concerning humankind, was a closed system. He also felt that to gain a profound understanding of humankind and life's central questions, one must explore the law of numbers. He believed everything was numerical and that there was nothing — our habits, likes, dislikes and personalities — that could not be explained by numbers. Seeing the great power underlying the law of numbers, he explored the notion that number holds divine harmony and power, and that in no other way could harmony or perfection be obtained. He defined in each number a principle: an active force of the universe.

Pythagoras is certainly not alone in his views. Eddington and Einstein amaze us with their teachings of a universe of exquisite numerical precision. And the symbolical relevance of numbers is generally accepted without question: 1 represents a unit; 2 immediately suggests the idea of duality, and so on. Down through the ages, even those who did not study numbers mystically, discerned in them more than meets the eye. Numbers may be the only vehicle via which our most advanced knowledge of the universe can be expressed.

Throughout this book, we will explore the vibrational influence of each number in various contexts, generally as applied to an individual: for example, as a ruling number, a day number, a personal year number, or a number within a chart.

The descriptions in this chapter explain the pure essence and symbolic relevance of each number, as well as their general characteristics in human terms.

INNER MEANINGS AND SYMBOLISM OF THE NUMBERS

Sir Thomas Browne (1605–1682), renowned British physician, philosopher and admirer of Pythagoras, wrote: 'All things began in order, so shall they end, so shall they begin again according to the Ordainer of Order and the mystical mathematics of the City of Heaven.'

1

The number 1 represents unity and is symbolised by the point:

•

Its vibration resonates with the life force that permeates everything. 1 relates to expression of the individual as a reflection of the universe and of all creation. It is ruled by the positive Sun.

In the Pythagorean method of numerology, 1 occurs in the ruling numbers 10 and 11, and in the day number of those born on the first day of any month, as well as appearing on individual birthdate, name and pyramid charts.

The number 1 vibrates to the colours of flame.

1 relates to issues of leadership and independence.

2

2 represents duality. It is symbolised by the line:

•————————•

It is the number of contrasts and opposites — good and evil, truth and error, heat and cold, dark and light, etcetera. By its very nature, it functions as a bridge or link, attracting all manner of other influences. Its dualistic influence is inclined to exhibit as a gentle, restless energy.

Number 2 is ruled by the negative moon.

It vibrates to the colour of gold.

2 relates to mediation, sensitivity and the desire for harmony.

3

3 is the number of the trinity. It is symbolised by the triangle, which Pythagoras called the surface:

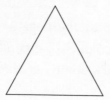

The number 3 represents the Grand Triunion: in Christian terms, the Father, Son and Holy Spirit; more generally, past, present and future; father, mother, child; spirit and matter, united by mind. It incorporates the vibrational influences of 1 and 2.

Number 3 is ruled by Jupiter.

It vibrates to the colour of flame and gold.

There are two distinct aspects to 3: creativity, positive good-humoured expression, optimism; or serene connection to the world of nature.

4

4, being the product of equals (2 x 2), signifies justice. It is symbolised by the square:

Pythagoreans called 4 the great miracle, taking their most sacred oaths over this number. For them, it was the foundation stone, the first of the solids from which all other solids are formed.

Number 4 is ruled by the negative Sun.

It vibrates to the colours of green and blue.

It is the number of stability, endurance, practicality and firmness of purpose.

5

5 represents expansion. Its symbol is the five-pointed star:

This symbol represents a human being standing in the centre of the universe, arms and legs outstretched, mind soaring to the highest realms. 5, therefore, is the number of humanity in which the spirit of life eternal and the spirit of intelligence and love combine.

Number 5 is ruled by Mercury.

It vibrates to the colour of pink.

5 rules the higher mind as well as inner desires, creativity and adaptability.

6

6 is the number of creation: the force behind nature and evolution. Its symbol is two triangles overlaid to create a six-pointed star:

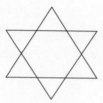

The two triangles of 6's symbol, pointing in opposite directions, indicate aspects of unrest and incompleteness, leading to the urge for completion, which occurs when the triangles form a perfect six-pointed star.

6 is ruled by Venus.

It vibrates to the colours of orange, scarlet and heliotrope.

Its influence vibrates with the thinker, the reasoner, the prophet and the 'cosmic mother' or helper of all beings.

7

7 represents the temple door. Its symbol is a triangle sitting on top of a square:

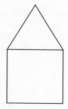

The temple door opens onto the mysteries of life, offering the experience of learning wisdom via the shattering of life's ideals.

7 is ruled by the positive Moon.

It vibrates to the colours of purple and steel grey.

The vibration of 7 resonates more with the spiritual than the physical realms; with mysticism and idealism; with illusion and disillusionment.

8

The number 8 has three different symbols: two squares; two triangles; and two circles.

The two squares represent independence:

The two triangles represent the hourglass, the balance of cause and effect, the perfect figure 8:

The two circles represent two worlds: the spiritual and the material:

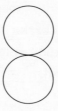

Clearly a complex number, 8 was called 'death' by the ancients because it requires a dying of the old to achieve evolution into a higher state of life. It operates under the principle of absolute justice and the element of fire which relentlessly purifies until only pure gold remains.

8 is ruled by Saturn.

It vibrates to the colours of canary and opal.

The number 8 resonates with karmic responsibilities, life lessons, structure and absolute integrity.

9

9 represents initiation via the trinity of trinities. Its symbol is two squares and the 1.

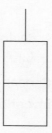

In 9, the 1 of leadership combines with the wisdom and challenges of 8, producing a vibration that brings things to an end and prepares for new manifestation. This vibration encourages humans to work for the good of all humanity, acting from an understanding of the unity of all life and the brotherhood of humankind.

9 is ruled by Mars.

It vibrates to the colours of red and brown.

The number 9 resonates with tolerance and empathy. Physical energy and effort provide the driving force for mental and emotional growth and development.

10

Like its first component, 1, the number 10 represents unity and creative force.

Ruled by the positive Sun, it embodies the element of fire with its capacity to burn out whatever physical aspects do not serve the highest good.

Like 1, it vibrates to the colour of flame.

11

The number 11 represents idealism, spirituality and faith.

As a power number, it vibrates to the frequencies of spiritual (natural) law, in resonance with material law. It is the symbol of genius, invention, independent thought and action.

Humans who are able to elevate themselves to live in resonance with 11 have the capacity to access the spiritual realms where all knowledge resides, thereby learning and applying universal truths for the benefit of all humanity.

11 vibrates to the colours of white, black, yellow and violet.

22

The inner meaning of 22 is similar to that of 11, but better able to adapt itself to the material world. 22 resonates more strongly with the conjunction of spirit and matter, lending itself to philanthropy in those who are able to resonate with its very high frequency.

22 is sometimes referred to as the master builder number, conferring the ability to ground high wisdom into practical reality.

It vibrates to the colour of cream.

33

This is the number of Creation, doubled. It is similar to the single number 6, but has deeper meaning with stronger energy and is referred to as the inspiration giving Master Teacher.

Like the 6, this number is ruled by Venus and vibrates to the colours of orange, scarlet and heliotrope.

The influence vibrates with the thinker, the reasoner, the prophet and the 'cosmic mother'.

Chapter 2

RULING NUMBERS, DAY NUMBERS AND PERSONAL YEAR NUMBERS

Many people are in ignorance of their true destinies and are striving for things that do not belong to them, and would only bring failure and dissatisfaction if attained.

THE GAME OF LIFE AND HOW TO PLAY IT, FLORENCE SCOVEL SHINN

An understanding of our ruling, day and personal year numbers can form a reassuring foundation for understanding our strengths and challenges in life. Each is influential in its own way, and can be considered along with other vibrational influences to provide insight and clarity in virtually any life context.

Ruling numbers

The ruling number is calculated from the numbers in one's birthdate and indicates those capabilities a person is born with. The ruling number influences everything a person does in life, so the knowledge of one's potential as disclosed by this ruling number enables an individual to plan the vibrational ebbs and flows.

As we go through life it is beneficial to refer to our ruling number, as a reminder, to ensure we are continuing on our most appropriate life path. This gives us reassurance.

In the Pythagorean method, there is no ruling number 1. The number 1 in the religious sense symbolises God, almighty and powerful. In a philosophical sense, it symbolises the fundamental unity of all things. 1 stands for our existence and represents the higher individual self — the self that is different from anyone else. The late Unity Church minister, author and speaker, Eric Butterworth, explained it this way: 'In the Pythagorean method of mathematics, Pythagoras deals with the idea that all numbers are reversible. They proceed from unity and they resolve back into unity. They all come out of One and they all resolve back into One.'

Although number 1 is not used as a ruling number, people born on the first day of the month do have 1 as their day number (see page 79). These people prefer to work alone.

The ruling number is a pervasive influence throughout one's life. However, remember that to fully understand the impact of numerology, we must consider all aspects of the chart. For example, there can be two or more children with the same ruling number in one family, but the differences will be found in the birthdate chart, the day number, their name chart and their month of birth.

In the case of twins or other multiple births, although they have the same birthdate numbers, the influences from their names and the path in life each chooses will ensure that they are still individuals with their own personality, opinions, taste, choices of colour, music and so on.

Environmental and cultural factors, gender, maturity and the capacity of human beings to exercise free will and choice all contribute to the way an individual lives out the details of their life. Just as there are positive and negative / light and dark aspects to all facets of creation, the vibrational influences of ruling numbers can be played out in a positive or negative fashion in one's day-to-day life, so positive and negative aspects are listed for each of the numbers. For most people, one will prevail but glimpses of the other will appear from time to time.

The numbers themselves are neither positive nor negative, but lifestyle, family or environmental factors can influence individuals to view life from a positive or negative perspective. Throughout our lives, most of us will fluctuate between the two, with a propensity to favour a positive viewpoint most of the time. We are all subject to the subtle pressures of everyday life. Consider this scenario: you are driving along a busy highway and you have just overtaken — say — six cars. Now, you're in front. Suddenly, you feel a need to maintain your speed and stay alert so that you do not annoy the drivers you've just passed by slowing them down. This is pressure. After a while, your concentration wanes, and a car comes seemingly out of nowhere and passes yours. Now, you can choose either to keep up with it or cruise comfortably and risk dropping back. Life can be like this when we are doing our best to stay positive: its subtle pressures can be complex and frequent.

Similarly, while exploring gender differentials might not be politically correct, there are primal differences in the personality and lifestyle traits that men and women tend towards; hence, the separate notes for each. These characteristics might melt or blend into each other, but will often be evident.

Ultimately, as humans, we have free will and choice. Regardless of external factors and our own strengths and limitations, in most situations we have a choice or choices. Sometimes we feel as though our choices have taken us on a side-track or even a back-track. But at any point, when faced with a choice, we can choose to head in a positive (or less negative) direction. In this sense, each of us controls his or her own destiny.

In the Pythagorean method there are 11 ruling numbers. They run from 2 through to 11, then a special number: 22/4. This is a second type of ruling number 4, but 22/4 is a master number, always referred to as 'twenty-two four'.

In the first edition of this book in 2007, there was no mention of the Ruling Number 33/6 as a Master Number. Now in 2015, eight years on, I have since researched the number 33/6 and along with other like-minded Numerologists, have concluded that 33/6 is indeed in the category of a Master Number.

Since adding that extra number [33/6] there are now 12 numbers in this Pythagorean Method, namely: ruling numbers 2 to 10 with three Master Numbers, 11, 22/4 and 33/6.

The ruling number 11 in this method is not reduced to the number 2 but remains as the number 11; as does 22/4, which is spoken as twenty-two four; and the 33/6, which is spoken as thirty-three six.

ODD AND EVEN RULING NUMBERS
People whose ruling number is odd (3, 5, 7, 9, and Master Number 11) have an overall tendency to exhibit lots of nervous energy. They are dynamic and proactive, prone to taking risks and capable of doing many seemingly dangerous things.

People ruled by an even number (2, 4, 6, 8, 10, and Master Numbers 22/4 and 33/6) are likely to be relatively placid. They are not easily aroused and generally seem to take things in their stride.

Those ruled by the number 8 have the fascinating capacity to exhibit traits characteristic of both odd and even groups.

CALCULATING RULING NUMBERS

Here are some examples showing how to calculate an individual's ruling number:

Birthdate: 10/12/1993.
Add each digit: $1 + 0 + 1 + 2 + 1 + 9 + 9 + 3 = 26$.
Then add $2 + 6 = 8$.
The ruling number is 8.

Birthdate: 3/1/1962.
Add each digit: $3 + 1 + 1 + 9 + 6 + 2 = 22$.
Then add $2 + 2 = 4$ (22/4).

This ruling number, 22/4, is not reduced and remains 22/4 — a master number.

Birthdate: 29/8/1954.
Add each digit: $2 + 9 + 8 + 1 + 9 + 5 + 4 = 38$.
Then add $3 + 8 = 11$.
The ruling number is 11.

Birthdate: 28/7/1982.
Add each digit: $2 + 8 + 7 + 1 + 9 + 8 + 2 = 37$.
Then add $3 + 7 = 10$.
The ruling number is 10.

Each ruling number, except for 2 and 22/4, can be calculated by adding different combinations of numbers. For example, ruling number 10 can be arrived at on the initial addition or by adding any of the following combinations:
19 (1 + 9); 28 (2 + 8); 37 (3 + 7); 46 (4 + 6).

RULING NUMBER 2
There is only one total in a birthdate that will add to a ruling number 2, and that is the total of 20.

Number 2 is a soul number, and these people receive great help through their intuition. They are very sensitive and are often looked upon as possessing a complex nature. Because 2 represents duality, ruling number 2 people are generally not comfortable working alone.

They are the peacemakers and honest plodders. They have to learn to mix with people to find their happiness. 2 is the number of deep emotion and those ruled by it feel everything very keenly. They are adaptable and like to be friends with everybody. Their progress may be slow but it is deliberate and definite.

Ruling number 2 people are tactful and diplomatic. They put a lot into life and get what they want by being clever. They also do a lot of giving and don't expect anything in return, and because of this can be taken for granted.

People vibrating to this number are imaginative, artistic and romantic. It is a number more of heart than of mind.

They are sympathetic, unselfish and capable of deep affection; pliant and yielding, they are easily influenced by other people. They can be over-sensitive, becoming desperately unhappy and despondent if disliked by those around them or if they are not in happy surroundings.

They dislike trouble and are kind, gentle, reliable, diligent and compassionate, possessing the important ability of peacemaker, sometimes to the extent of being reformers.

Ruling number 2s are less motivated by ego than most people, exhibiting the selfless and noble acumen of merging their ego with that of their associates when desirable or necessary.

They must be allowed to progress at their own natural pace and they prefer to consolidate as they go. They are exceptionally honourable and dislike their integrity being doubted, as this can undermine their confidence.

The number 2 is the symbol of duality. Sometimes those ruled by it are capable and confident and other times they are reserved and shy. The number 2 will draw a great diversity of experiences to those who are ruled by it. People vibrating to 2 will link their lives with a wide range of individuals and conditions. They are easily moulded and will slip into situations just as water moulds itself into a square or round pan. They have the 'mother' nature, are intuitive and have a temperament so fine they are not well equipped to be independent in a fast, harsh environment.

Many arbitrators are found under the number 2. It creates a bridge, a link between people. They are likely to have natural psychic powers, as this figure gives clairvoyance: the ability to sense vibrations of the astral planes. It sometimes facilitates trance conditions.

The whole existence of people governed by this number is often coloured by their surroundings. The dualistic effect of the influence is inclined to cause a constant subtle warfare between reason and intuition that can show itself in restlessness, uncertainty, lack of continuity in plans and ideas, and in a lack of confidence.

POSITIVE NUMBER 2

These people never intentionally offend. They are peacemakers, gentle, plodders, very sensitive and capable of feeling deep emotion. They are definite in their likes and dislikes but exhibit great understanding and consideration for others. They love peace and can be difficult to rouse to argument. They are tactful and obliging, harmonious and imaginative, refined and artistic. They love to be with people because it makes them happy and they thrive in congenial surroundings. Usually the heart rules the head.

NEGATIVE NUMBER 2

These people are purposeless and weak — mostly afraid of public opinion, untruthful, shifty and selfish. They will be nice to your face but make derogatory remarks about you in your absence. Because of their over-sensitivity they can be introverted and moody, although if they become aware of this they can find happiness in learning how to mix.

RULING NUMBER 2 WOMEN

Within themselves they often feel unimportant and if they hang onto this negative thought they receive very little from life. Only through association with true friends can they really become known. Obscurity is their keynote, yet they can be a harmonising influence in a crowd. They follow but never lead (except in situations where they know their subject well and feel confident). They often attract dominant men, and because of this quality men say, 'She helps me feel at peace and asks nothing in return.'

The ruling number 2 woman's governing passion is adaptability. It is said she teaches the spirit of gentleness.

RULING NUMBER 2 MEN

They are strong in some ways and weak in others, but in their friendships they are sincere. Being sensitive they seek peace, sometimes at great cost to themselves. Their married life is usually successful because they are diplomatic. If they are able to access it, they will find great strength and power within themselves. They are only happy in certain company. They are natural fathers and devoted to home life. They are easily hurt and sometimes think deeply before they can forgive. They are good diplomats in all walks of life.

RULING NUMBER 2 CHILDREN

Children with this ruling number are super-sensitive and have super-understanding. They know immediately whether mum or dad means a smile or a frown. If they feel they are misjudged or wilfully neglected they become disobedient and will withstand threats and scoldings. If they tell lies it will only be as a protection for themselves and never with any malicious intention. These children love peace and harmony so much that if a misunderstanding parent misjudges them, for the sake of peace, they will tell a lie. Parents really need to understand this. In fact, right through life they are never found in serious or wilful wrong intent. If you catch them out in a lie, talk it over with them and you will discover the reason. Don't scold them before you talk with them.

These children are kind, friendly, and happiest among other children. Sometimes they are capable and confident, other times reserved and shy. It will help them a lot if they are encouraged to express their ideas. Give credit to these children whenever possible as this will develop their confidence. When they grow older it is advisable for them to work with other people. They are lovers of art, nature and all beauty and will do well in any area where they can use their creativity.

These children may be quiet and shy. They often wish to play alone and can be very happy. But it is wise to encourage them to mix with other children as well.

The possible early inclination to reticence can be overcome by understanding parents, by patience and encouragement of these children to express themselves in their own way. Once they have been ridiculed they take a long time to recover. If a number 2 child appears quiet or withdrawn and the parent reacts with irritability, the child's development can be set back, possibly for years.

HARMONISING MONTHS FOR RULING NUMBER 2 PEOPLE

These months are the most powerful for major happenings in the life of a ruling 2 person: February (2), April (4), August (8).

SOME SUITABLE VOCATIONS FOR RULING NUMBER 2 PEOPLE

Personal assistants to administrators; personal assistants in charitable organisations; working in areas of education; psychoanalysts or psychologists; social workers; diplomats; secretaries; counsellors. Most ruling number 2 people feel more comfortable working as part of a group. They are good writers, musicians and teachers who work harmoniously with others.

POSSIBLE HEALTH ISSUES FOR RULING NUMBER 2 PEOPLE

They have weak stomachs and need a plain strengthening diet. They may develop digestive troubles brought on through sensitivity and by not being understood. Look after the bowels as there could later be obstructions.

RULING NUMBER 3

The following are special characteristics of each combination of birthdate totals for ruling number 3 people.

12/3 These people suffer a loneliness of some kind. They feel separated and something sad happens to hurt them deeply.

21/3   Intuition guides them in everything they do. They are self-conscious and always striving to please. They meet a fair amount of trouble.

30/3   This number is joined to the circle of mysticism. More or less during their lives, these people are associated with spiritual affairs and have a natural psychic ability.

39/3   They have the power to lead and to express the true self but often find themselves burdened with trials and responsibilities. They possess psychic ability but can be very restless.

There are two distinct types of any ruling number 3 people:

- expressive, bubbly, optimistic, with a good imagination and a love of colourful clothes
- the quiet ruling number 3 people who love the countryside and nature and prefer a more reserved dress code

3 is a mind plane number, a mystic figure which is related to matters of religion, spirituality, science and philosophy. Most ruling 3 people have natural psychic powers, and many will be associated with religious/spiritual affairs at some time in their lives. It is also a number associated with art, music, beauty, entertainment, literature, joy and ease.

Ruling number 3 people are quick-thinking. Their mental alertness is sometimes expressed in a keen sense of humour. Their active brain often means success in their working life and among their social contacts. This attribute does not always show in their home life as they can be critical, and this can be wearing on those closest to them.

Wherever it occurs, the number 3 is the vibration of expression. Most musicians, actors, artists, writers and other creatives vibrate to one of the numbers divisible by three — whether it is the day or ruling number that is 3, 6 or 9. The mission of the number 3 person is to be happy and make others happy.

This number is a combination of the numbers 1 and 2. It produces a many-sided nature with the ability to please, and to swing with the crowd. These people make excellent hosts.

The ambition of some ruling number 3 people is to have control and authority over others. They are proud and independent and don't want to feel obliged to anyone. Unless the ruling number 3 person finds their true course, theirs can be an aimless life.

Humour is one of the most important qualities of this vibration. Ruling number 3s have the light touch in life. They exhibit an innate light-hearted quality of spirit that nothing can subdue — which is just as well, since ruling 3 frequently brings difficulties and trials as well. Often, these occur as a result of circumstances over which the individual has no control.

POSITIVE NUMBER 3

These people can be inspirationally musical or artistic. They are always ready to give of themselves for the upliftment of others and if they choose, can be accomplished in almost any field of the arts and entertainment. They are self-expressive, bubbly, happy and optimistic, and have a good imagination. They also have the ability to bring happiness and joy and are very conscious of the feelings of others.

NEGATIVE NUMBER 3
Such people are selfish, discordant, self-satisfied, ambitious, impatient, and scatter their mental forces. They can be precise and self-righteous and a source of worry to their friends and family. They can be extravagant and vain, dogmatic and narrow-minded.

RULING NUMBER 3 WOMEN
These women love life and pleasure, and are usually marvellous hosts and entertainers. They expect others to join them in their celebration of life and liberty. If constructive, they will make every effort to help wherever possible. Ruling 3 women never hold deep grudges, and strongly resent injustice. They make fine friends and do not expect more from life than they put into it. They are usually bright people and their company is welcome.

RULING NUMBER 3 MEN
These men are happy people ready for anything life has to offer. They might scatter their forces, making it difficult for them to achieve their aims. They can sometimes be down but never out. They are not afraid, and in the face of adversity, they simply wait and gather themselves together

again. These men never ask too much in return for anything they do.

They often marry very young, and if they are unhappy they make the best of it. If they do not marry or live with a partner they will interest themselves in someone else's home — possibly their mother's.

Ruling 3 men are deeply compassionate and, if they train their inspirational powers toward philosophical teachings, they can help humanity. There is courage in their hearts under all circumstances. If they wish, they can make good public entertainers.

RULING NUMBER 3 CHILDREN

Children with this ruling number have strong mind power, keen intuition and an inner strength which is always on the defensive.

Many talk a great deal, while others express themselves in drawings or making different objects. These children must be well disciplined; otherwise, they become domineering and will stand up against their parents. They are usually bright and happy, and love good clothes. Some of them become upset or develop stomach upsets if they are deprived of the happy or pretty things in life.

Encourage them to enter into outdoor sports which burn up nervous energy and strengthen the powers of concentration.

Watch that they don't become critical and intolerant. They need something to constantly hold their interest. Be aware, though, that these children can drive themselves needlessly and end up exhausted. Give them 'time out' for rest periods. They also need plenty of sleep.

They are capable of very deep love and can be helped if they feel loved and understood in return.

Some of these children will display interests in electrical or mechanical things, music or some form of light entertainment. Others follow spiritual or religious teachings.

There are also the quieter types of ruling 3 children who love the countryside and open spaces, and feel that they must have freedom. They will express themselves in their 'work' or in some hobby or interest they cultivate. They love being surrounded by nature and generally find satisfaction and delight in the beauties of life, whether in the natural world or among their friends.

The type of 3 to which a child belongs will be very evident.

HARMONISING MONTHS FOR RULING NUMBER 3 PEOPLE

These months are the most powerful for major happenings in the life of a ruling 3 person: March (3), June (6), September (9), December (12/3).

SOME SUITABLE VOCATIONS FOR RULING NUMBER 3 PEOPLE

Business managers; any of the sciences; academic fields; medicine; accountants; computer programmers; electrical interests, mechanical interests; actors, entertainers, musicians, singers, dancers, painters; writers; critics; teachers. They do well in any position that involves a degree of freedom and meeting others.

POSSIBLE HEALTH ISSUES FOR RULING NUMBER 3 PEOPLE
These people suffer from over-strain of the nervous system. They drive themselves, often without cause, and can end up with neuritis or sciatica and, sometimes, skin troubles.

RULING NUMBER 4
The following are special characteristics of each combination of birthdate totals for ruling number 4 people.

4   An example giving this birthdate total would be 1/1/2000. These people will find life very frustrating and confining.

13/4   These people are very highly strung and often experience suppression that does not allow them to express themselves.

22/4   This is a ruling number in its own right. See page 74.

31/4   If these people enter into mysticism they should be very careful. It is always wise for them to stay on terra firma; this also applies to those with this day number. They should not delve too far into psychic studies.

40/4   A very complex combination, mystical and practical. They are often confused between the spiritual and the material. They are either very matter-of-fact or dreamers. These people can write well.

Ruling number 4 people are the defenders of home and country. If raised in a positive environment, they are utterly trustworthy and not easily swayed. They make up the rank and file of the world. They are critical, discerning and filled with unrest and ambition. They work hard for their money, and naturally hoard and save. They are found in the midst of the fray, and are the active ones. These people form business partnerships, are organisers and managers. 4s are practical people and, as work is the foundation of human life, they are practical workers.

This is a number given to analysis and discussion. These people are positive, liking to know the reason for all things. They are not swayed by talk, are level-headed and not given to sentiment. They are not afraid of personal work, and will reach the height of their inner powers. They can be relied on for management, endurance and faithfulness to duty.

Since the number 4 deals with the intellect and practical matters, these people assess everything from a logical perspective, usually demanding a clear, literal translation or interpretation. The true 4 works with the mind and the hands. 4 means construction, building, work and service. It is a substantial and heavy earth plane vibration: the number of order, law, arrangement, medium level leadership, poise and balance.

The number 4 gives the tendency to plod — to stay in one groove, to remain a long time in one environment. It usually means these people are good friends who attract good opportunities, although those who are too strongly influenced by their ruling 4 do not always take advantage of opportunities because they lack initiative. However, if there is only one 4 in the birthdate and it is fortified with other numbers which make for progress, then success in life is assured.

A word of caution: because of their tendency to work long hours, ruling 4 people can neglect their loved ones. They have a prevailing urge to keep on working, to the extent that they may not know how to relax. It is wise for ruling 4 people to make a point of taking time off (even if it is only for a weekend). This will help keep them and their relationships healthy. Ruling 4 people who do not heed this advice can find their marriage or partnership comes under severe strain, even to the point of separation or divorce, because they are so entirely focused on work.

This number gives strength and vitality to the physical body and those ruled by it recuperate quickly, recovering strength and vitality that may have been lost through illness.

Ruling number 4 people are the backbone of commerce (in a different way to ruling number 8 people). Others may come and go, but of the 4 we often say: 'He restored my faith in humanity.'

POSITIVE NUMBER 4

These people like being of service, are the mechanical workers, are kind and reliable. With their strong sense of what is right, they pay attention to detail, have physical endurance, enjoy planning and are good solid matter-of-fact people. Practical, honest, conscientious and loyal, they like to feel secure. Positive number 4s might consider emotional people weak, but are dependable friends who thrive on encouragement from their partners.

NEGATIVE NUMBER 4
These people must guard against becoming dogmatic, narrow minded and repressive. With a tendency to be set in their opinions, they do not like flighty people and their dislike often shows. This negative side of the 4 can be crude and dissatisfied. They have contempt for refinement and learning and give uncheerful service. These people are the clock-watchers, the drudges, the agitators, and complaining wives or husbands.

RULING NUMBER 4 WOMEN
Women ruled by 4 are strong and plain-spoken, but so very loving underneath. At times they might appear distant, particularly if they feel someone is belittling them, yet they give generously and expect appreciation in return. In their home these women are likely to be self-sacrificing and do too much, although this can change if they feel someone else receives greater favour. They never accept defeat easily and although they might appear indifferent, there are not many people who realise a situation more readily or who suffer so deeply.

RULING NUMBER 4 MEN

Solid earth people who command respect, these men are often forced by circumstances to become a support for many. They discipline themselves and like to discipline others, often considering themselves judge and jury. They are fond of their home and if necessary will struggle to provide the best of everything for the ones they love.

These men are industrious rather than sentimental or demonstrative. They are faithful to their friends and to employees if they have them. A number 4 man is a constant husband who will often marry a woman of opposite tendencies; in such situations, she might long after a while to live on her own and to allow her plodding husband to live alone as well.

RULING NUMBER 4 CHILDREN

Children ruled by this practical number want to know the reason for all things. They are not easy to train and can become defiant if ordered about. Never speak harshly to them. Speaking to them in a kindly manner will allow parents to handle them much more easily. If they feel misunderstood they fly into tantrums and remain upset for a long time. These children will listen to patient, thorough explanations.

If number 4 children feel trusted, they will give their best. They are dependable and love to please, responding positively to appreciation. Encourage them to write stories.

This is a sure way of helping to unfold their strong, loving natures. Although number 4 children find it difficult to be demonstrative, they are always sincere. Their first impressions are generally right and if this aspect is respected, life will flow smoothly. In other words, if these children have a 'feeling' about something, listen attentively to what they have to say.

Because they have potential managerial and supervisory qualities, number 4s like to boss other children. If they become too upset, they are inclined to melancholia.

HARMONISING MONTHS FOR RULING NUMBER 4 PEOPLE

These months are the most powerful for major happenings in the life of a ruling 4 person: February (2), April (4), August (8).

SOME SUITABLE VOCATIONS FOR RULING NUMBER 4 PEOPLE

Managers; economists; physicians; technicians; machinists; skilled trades people; mechanics; technical instructors; members of the armed services. They are efficient, compassionate workers with an occasional tendency to be considered abrupt or gruff in the way they relate to their clients or staff.

POSSIBLE HEALTH ISSUES FOR RULING NUMBER 4 PEOPLE

These people suffer with ailments that are sometimes difficult to describe. They are inclined to melancholia and a very discontented mind, which can result in headaches, kidney, liver and bladder troubles.

RULING NUMBER 5

The following are special characteristics of each combination of birthdate totals for ruling number 5 people.

5   An example giving this birthdate total would be 1/10/2001. These people must have strong direction in their lives from a very early age in order to thrive.

14/5   They may carry heavy burdens and experience very little freedom.

23/5   This is a combination of soul and mind, often responsible for inner conflict; they sometimes hurt others unintentionally.

32/5   A well-balanced total. Such a person is often thought to have a dual nature. They are often found to be leaders in the world of art and medicine; in fact, in any area where they can be leaders and innovators.

41/5   Always practical in some way; a very different 5 from the 23/5 or 32/5. Many find contentment in an office but must have the lead. These people have a strong personality.

The central soul number, 5 is dynamic. It is the centre of the will, and empowers people to get things done and carry things through. Ruling number 5s are versatile people. They like freedom, love change, generally lack a sense of responsibility and dislike obligation and rule, but are generous, good-natured and forgiving. If number 5 people live at their highest potential they will generally know the thoughts of others. They are mostly self-sufficient, well poised, fascinating and charming. If any unpleasantness arises, they seldom injure or hate, but simply turn their thoughts in another direction. Under a 5 vibration, people may often simply 'fall into' a marriage or romantic partnership. Money comes and goes and the wheel of life turns so rapidly that they are often forced to wonder what the next event will be. If they are living in their true vibration they will accept each experience and learn from it.

To concentrate or to go into the silence is the safeguard of this vibration. A regular meditation practice serves them very well. These people are mentally very highly strung and quick in thought and decision. They are impulsive in action and their greatest drawback is that they exhaust their mental strength to such an extent that they often fall victim to stress, easily becoming irritable and quick tempered.

5 is the number of extremes and produces restlessness. It can be a beneficial influence when the person lives in moderation, but if they live in extremes, the strength of the 5 is likely to weaken their will, making them seem unreliable. People influenced by this number are sympathetic and kind but easily led, unless there are other numbers in the birthdate

that are strong and firm. Their intuition is their greatest asset and they often hit upon the right thing at the right time, but they do not like to pay attention to detail. As a result, while their intentions are good, they often find themselves in trouble.

Number 5 people are exactly opposite in their nature to the number 4 people — the plodders and workers; freedom-loving number 5 people are often referred to as the 'youth of the world' because of their light-hearted attitude.

Ruling number 5s are leaders, and do not generally work successfully for a boss — unless they work in conditions where they can be free to make some of the decisions and present their own ideas.

POSITIVE NUMBER 5

These people stand for freedom, liberty, justice and originality. They are adaptable, versatile, loving and generous. Inspirational, intuitive and ambitious, they will meet life with open arms, aiming to achieve unity with every experience as a means for higher development of the self.

NEGATIVE NUMBER 5

These people are characterised by self-indulgence, confusion and quarrels. They may very easily fall into situations of complete failure and waste, sinking to any excess without thinking of the consequences. They seek to gratify the desires of the moment and can be shifty and unreliable. Also, they procrastinate and cannot be depended on to do well.

Negative number 5s resist change concerning issues in their personal life, and can miss opportunities by holding onto things for too long.

RULING NUMBER 5 WOMEN
These women are changeable and love luxury and finery. If things become too slow for them they may feel that their spirit of liberty is being constricted. They are neither dull nor dogmatic but even so, to function at their best, must be allowed to feel free. A few like to gamble, but if they take chances they are usually good losers.

RULING NUMBER 5 MEN
These men need structure in their lives. They are the epitome of restlessness and love change. They are sensitive and touchy to any criticism. These men are known to many as the 'lovers' of the world. They crave freedom, sometimes seeming immune to time. They really love their home and family yet can easily leave, always expecting to return. If they become hot-headed, they are impossible to reason with at that moment. They can make promises with the best of intentions but just as easily break them. At heart, they are gamblers with life, loving anything that offers a quick return. They can be the life of any party or gathering, and their personality and ease pleases everyone. They make good friends and bad enemies. Through their love of change, they can create unhappy homes.

RULING NUMBER 5 CHILDREN

Children with this powerful number are restless, excitable and lovers of adventure. They are very determined and will go the long way round to gain their point. They love freedom, and parents may find it difficult to tie them down. A garden of their own or a pet will help considerably.

Generally, these kind-hearted children are not aware of restrictions, and can be forever getting into all kinds of mischief. However, they are very creative and take a keen interest in everything they do; given the right opportunities these children can become good students. Without clear boundaries and routines, they can become wild and uncontrollable. Parents who communicate with firm, gentle kindness to establish agreed parameters will fare best. Number 5 children are always ready to help, but will very quickly become selfish if they feel boxed in.

These children are attractive and have an appealing manner. They are usually artistic, creative and may be good at writing. Their strong, freedom-loving spirits thrive when allowed to express themselves in constructive, creative pursuits.

If they are unhappy at home, they leave as soon as possible, yet the love of home is very strong.

HARMONISING MONTHS FOR RULING NUMBER 5 PEOPLE

These months are the most powerful for major happenings in the life of a ruling 5 person: May (5), October (10).

SOME SUITABLE VOCATIONS FOR RULING NUMBER 5 PEOPLE

Doctors; engineers; designers; salespeople; decorators; any of the arts; journalists/writers; marine workers; inventors.

POSSIBLE HEALTH ISSUES FOR RULING NUMBER 5 PEOPLE

These people live on their nerves — mentally and physically. This can bring on neuritis, nervous twitches and even paralysis. Sleep and rest, and lots of it, are necessary. Avoid administering drugs.

RULING NUMBER 6

The following are special characteristics of each combination of birthdate totals for ruling number 6 people.

6   These people must exercise great strength of character to enable them to have some happiness. They will worry far too much.

15/6   These people desire to lead but have little opportunity presented to them.

24/6   They will experience some opposition to all their soul's desires if grasping for things of an earthly nature.

33/6   This is a marvellous total with unlimited power and is a ruling number in its own right.

42/6   This is a strong combination if there is no 8 in the birthdate. They are able to take on leadership, handle people, organise big companies and undertake business deals. Anything they undertake is done well.

Ruling number 6 people are creative, caring, just, unselfish, tolerant and home-loving. But they are inclined toward deep worry and extreme anxiety. These people are often too cautious for their own good. This can cause them to become cynical, disbelieving and suspicious.

They have good reasoning ability and a quick wit, are broad-minded and able to take a comprehensive mental grasp of any situation very rapidly.

To achieve success it is necessary for number 6 people to concentrate. This also keeps them in good health as their metabolism is often upset. They often serve the people and are excellent as heads of institutions or businesses, especially in foodstuffs (because of their urge to nurture). These people are generally good at figures. They are neat, and love order in just about everything they do. They are also great humanitarians.

Number 6 people must watch that they do not shirk their responsibilities and become the opposite of the true 6. At the same time, they need to take care not to make slaves of themselves in the home or in business. These people are true friends in need and comforters of the suffering, as well as being peacemakers and artists in the home.

POSITIVE NUMBER 6
These people are the thinkers and comforters, giving willing and cheerful service. They are conscientious and dependable,

born home-makers, optimistic, peace-loving and tolerant. If the need arises they fight valiantly for their principles. They could be compared to the salt of the earth and the backbone of the community — those who attract others to them and are much loved.

NEGATIVE NUMBER 6
These people are busybodies and gossips with so few interests that they are forever poking into the affairs of other people. They are sceptical, cynical and critical, narrow and uncharitable in their judgment. These people are generally overworked and never seem to accomplish anything. They are obstinate and untidy.

RULING NUMBER 6 WOMEN
These women love their home, motherhood and the garden. In the home they reign in the hearts of those they love. These people would rather be helpful than great. When they are positive they have a pleasing personality and their kind thoughts can make others happy. They care for anyone who is ill or in trouble.

RULING NUMBER 6 MEN
These men are the opposite of the number 5 men: they are naturally the marrying type. They are generous, honest and trustworthy, fond of ease and the comforts of life. Many of them enjoy music and singing at home with family and friends, and if their lifestyle is conducive may even become

public entertainers. But deep in their hearts, they are home bodies who love their own fireside.

RULING NUMBER 6 CHILDREN

Ruling number 6 children are the home-lovers, ready to help, especially if appreciated. If the home is an unhappy one or they are under the impression that their parents do not love them, they look for outside companions, and this leads many of them into trouble. Parents must make sure these children know they are loved, and are an integral part of the home.

They can easily become nervous and fretful, and if this happens, they become distrustful and develop an over-cautiousness, which spoils their nature.

Number 6 children are easy to deal with via love and kindness, yet can become problematic through lack of understanding. They have pleasant voices and love music, which is essential in their lives. This becomes a valuable avenue for self-expression, which helps the nervous system. If these children fret too much they lose their confidence, which is difficult for them to regain.

They love bright, artistic surroundings and if at all possible, should be well educated, as they are good with figures, bookkeeping and engineering. Number 6 children are fond of animals. They have original, creative abilities: drama class can help to keep them happy. Sincere appreciation means a lot to these people, as children and as adults.

HARMONISING MONTHS FOR RULING NUMBER 6 PEOPLE

These months are the most powerful for major happenings in the life of a ruling 6 person: March (3), June (6), September (9), December (12/3).

SOME SUITABLE VOCATIONS FOR RULING NUMBER 6 PEOPLE

Veterinary surgeons; doctors; nurses; teachers; real estate agents; humanitarians; healers; any of the arts; singers; actors; designers; heads of institutions or businesses, especially in foodstuffs.

POSSIBLE HEALTH ISSUES FOR RULING NUMBER 6 PEOPLE

They often have irregular circulation of the blood, which can affect the heart. Worry is mainly responsible for this. Exercise is an excellent remedy. Women often suffer with mastitis after childbirth, very often due to lack of sufficient exercise. The throat and upper part of the lungs are sometimes weak. Deep breathing and some outdoor activity can help overcome these problems.

RULING NUMBER 7

The following are special characteristics of each combination of birthdate totals of ruling number 7 people.

7   These people will know many sacrifices, and are often misunderstood.

16/7   All kinds of sadness comes into their home life and they often find themselves bearing the responsibilities of the home or family.

25/7   This is a very strong combination. They are often prophetic and very sensitive, and as a result can experience many trials and challenges in life.

34/7   They are found to be excellent people. They have the power of organisation with psychic power behind it, but very often are not given credit for their work.

43/7   This is a more emotional person, with keen power to discern, yet they have great strength of character. They experience their fair share of trials and tribulations.

The number 7 represents completion and understanding and is considered a sacred, mystical and spiritual number. Ruling number 7 people are strong and determined, often finding it difficult to accept discipline. They are born to be leaders, and if they do not find fulfilment at this level, can turn to some form of stimulant. Although they are ruled by an earth number, they often misrepresent themselves or feel misunderstood because of the mystical qualities associated with 7.

They present an exterior of extreme frankness and pleasantness but they always remain a partial mystery no matter how dearly they might love another. They naturally hold themselves apart from other people. For these reasons, ruling number 7 people can be unsatisfactory partners. They can appear lonely and misunderstood; such people are rarely appreciated at their full worth.

Ruling number 7 people tend to have a refined presence about them. They will always be able to do any kind of work set before them and will do it in a professional manner.

7 is the number of the mystic, the stoic, the priest and the religionist. It is the number of silence, non-expression, self-reliance, meditation, wisdom and understanding. Service and trial play a great part in the lives of these people and through this they find inner power, strength and endurance.

The true 7 can live alone and not be lonely. They have great power of attraction through the law of silence. Because this is also the number of overcoming and sacrifice, people ruled by 7 usually have a difficult early life. Later, they can become successful by reason of the experiences through which they have passed and from which they have learned. They may be hasty and rebellious, but they never give in to adverse circumstances and will fight to the last.

Number 7 people must guard against restlessness and becoming too sensitive. They must resist fear of failure and also a tendency to suppress people and to dominate. Occasionally, they fall into melancholy moods and can then be pessimistic. All of these things undo their power. Optimism is one thing they must learn.

Ruling number 7 people have mental strength and determination but physically they are not strong. They learn best by their own mistakes, therefore are self-teachers.

They can be highly inspirational, thriving on responsibility and shining as comforters, leaders, teachers and writers. They are successful in positions of trust. They are found amongst the most active in all walks of life, but to achieve their best they must also have peace and harmony. Therefore, until they reach a time in their lives when they can access these qualities, they find life difficult, and sometimes sad and trying.

These people should never try to be like others. In the silence they find peace, power and repose; this will draw people to them.

POSITIVE NUMBER 7
Positive number 7 people have wisdom, silence, poise, beauty of spirit, and can be alone yet rarely feel lonely. They are fastidious, refined, sensitive, and have infinite gentleness and poetry hidden in their nature.

NEGATIVE NUMBER 7
These people are turbulent, unreasonable, suspicious, jealous, lonely, argumentative and unable to retain friends. They tend to criticise everyone. They also insist on making everyone around them conform to their way of thinking, and wound the sensibilities of others.

RULING NUMBER 7 WOMEN
These women present either as very silent or the entertaining lady. Whatever they do, they feel apart, as though they are outside looking in. Their quietness is sometimes mistaken for weakness, but in fact they have a deep mental strength. If negative, they create a wall between themselves and others

because of their capacity to be natural hermits. These women have to be known to be understood. They dislike noise and confusion, preferring to plan their own lives; if left to do so, they handle life graciously, rarely making mistakes. If they do make mistakes they always learn by them.

RULING NUMBER 7 MEN

These men can be difficult to understand. They are silent, separate and introspective. They are natural philosophers, have keen insight, and yet are inclined to take too much for granted. If they lose heart some may seek solace in gambling, alcohol or some form of stimulant. They find happiness as teachers and by being comforters of other people. They are never tied to any creed even if they lose their own identity. They are meant to leave some message to the people, therefore should learn to lead. They suffer a great deal if misunderstood. A 7 man can be a splendid friend, looking for little in return.

RULING NUMBER 7 CHILDREN

Children with this vibrational strength are not easy to train or understand. They are born to lead and do not take kindly to discipline or any form of suppression. They learn by their mistakes. Love is their only conqueror.

Although it might not be apparent, 7s are very sensitive children, so never ridicule them; rather, encourage them wherever possible. Take them into your confidence and they will serve you faithfully. Many of them have sadness in early life and sacrifice plays a big part at some stage. They suffer deeply through this and life becomes difficult for them; then they feel lonely and yearn to escape their troubles.

For best results, never speak harshly to these children, and never draw their attention to anything you do not wish them to do, because their curiosity is aroused and they promptly disobey. These children have keen understanding, so take time to explain things and they will obey. If parents chastise them when they know they've done wrong, most number 7 children will accept the discipline without objection. They need a good education to enable them to take the lead in whatever they choose to do, otherwise they do very little with their strong talents.

These children will most likely be drawn to the public in various ways and can become very successful teachers of any subject. Properly trained, they have the strength to master anything they care to follow.

HARMONISING MONTHS FOR RULING NUMBER 7 PEOPLE
These months are the most powerful for major happenings in the life of a ruling 7 person: April (4), July (7), November (11).

SOME SUITABLE VOCATIONS FOR RULING NUMBER 7 PEOPLE
Engineers; scientists; teachers; inventors; artists in all forms; doctors; nurses; real estate agents; musicians; people in positions of trust.

POSSIBLE HEALTH ISSUES FOR RULING NUMBER 7 PEOPLE
Worry or annoyance easily upsets these people. This can bring
on bowel and stomach troubles. 7 people are stronger mentally
than physically. They are extremely sensitive and sometimes
melancholy. At some stage they will have skin problems.

Ruling number 8
The following are special characteristics of each combination
of birthdate totals for ruling number 8 people.

8   These people will find life very troublesome and will
         also find it difficult to assert their independence.
         They may feel isolated.

17/8   These people experience sorrow of a deep nature,
         perhaps in sickness and accidents.

26/8   These people demonstrate keen understanding in
         their homes but do not miss out on having home
         worries. They often find themselves involved with
         business or societies.

35/8   This is a combination of mind and soul with
         marvellous qualities of both. They are meant to lead
         and go forth into the public world. They often meet
         great sorrow in their private lives because 35 includes
         the soul number, 5.

44/8   This total exhibits in either a very crushed spirit or a
         very dominant personality (either extreme is possible,
         depending on the chart and the life choices of the

individual). They can only be helped with love and kindness. They make dependable friends and have been known to be very capable.

8 is the number of power, freedom, intuition, inspiration and intellect. It is also the number of the master consciousness in business, the practical number and the number of prosperous attainment. These people are very independent and also very sensitive, strongly resenting any interference in their plans. This can cause many misunderstandings.

A ruling 8 person has spiritual power when their desire is unselfish. Money will always come to satisfy their needs as long as they make themselves useful in the community. When they are seeking for others the blessings they seek for themselves, working for the race and not for the individual and looking for no return, then success is assured.

Because the planet Saturn — the planet of fate — rules number 8 people, this can be a difficult number to explain. Like the two circles just touching that compose it, it represents two worlds: the material and the spiritual. One circle or aspect of the number represents upheaval, revolution, waywardness, eccentricities of all kinds, strife, separation and destruction. The other circle or aspect represents philosophical thought, religious/spiritual devotion, and zealous concentration of purpose for any cause espoused to progressive harmony. The number 8 gives great psychic ability, sympathy, kindness, love of children and animals, as well as love for music, social life and change.

These people are poised, have strong willpower and can face difficulties calmly with assurance of success. They have self-confidence and things come their way. They dress well and usually look well in anything they choose to wear. They look prosperous and there is always an inner urge that drives towards prosperity.

These people do best when left to carry out their own ideas and plans. They resent any interference, regarding their independence as one of the most important aspects of life.

They are practical and can be hard if they lack awareness; this can cause misunderstandings. They like to help others but often express themselves in the wrong way because of their forceful spirit. They are able to carry out business schemes well and they possess good financial ability. They have the capacity to reconstruct a difficult problem and have exceptionally clear vision if left to follow their own intuition.

Number 8 people are prone to drive or push others, although they resent being driven themselves. They must also watch that they do not become too absorbed in business, resulting in neglect in their homes and to their loved ones. If this occurs it will cause a lot of sadness, yet they are the last ones to realise their mistake. Limitations of their power make them unhappy: they feel they must be allowed to express themselves in their own way; then they can attain any height.

These people are dependable friends. If they cannot express their feelings in words, they often buy a gift or do something practical to show how they feel. Idealists in love, they seek the perfect partnership, sometimes to the extent that they wander away from their life path in search of the perfect love. They can go through a long string of partners before they settle down, but if they marry, they are deep lovers of their home and family.

POSITIVE NUMBER 8
These people have power, constructive capacity, universal sympathy and understanding. This is a fine, forthright and brilliant number, yielding a loving and powerful person. They are sympathetic, kind and a great success, unselfishly living for others, desiring the truth in every phase of life. They are scrupulous and clear-sighted.

NEGATIVE NUMBER 8
These people misuse their power. They are strong in destruction, unsuccessful through misdirected strength, consummate scoundrels who live for self alone, acknowledging no law but their own wit. They oppress and crush and walk roughshod over others for the sheer love of asserting themselves. They become miserable failures.

RULING NUMBER 8 WOMEN
These women are strong and positive in their decisions and radiate courage to others. They have powerful leadership qualities and, in asserting themselves, can create misunderstandings. They have a tendency to take too much for

granted. They take exception to any interference in whatever they happen to be doing.

They have to learn to give and take; life is never perfect. Number 8 women are often the mothers of clever children and sacrifice themselves to help their offspring reach their goals. They admire strength of character and can show it in return. Their greatest craving is to be loved for themselves, although they realise that money too is a vital necessity. When they marry for love, they help their partner all the way.

RULING NUMBER 8 MEN

This is a powerful vibration. These men are often alone and often feel lonely. They are the great directors and have almost perfect judgment in financial or executive positions.

Their love powers are often hidden. They find it difficult to put into words just what they feel; therefore they are branded cold and calculating by many. They are happiest in the financial world.

RULING NUMBER 8 CHILDREN

Ruling number 8 children have the spirit of independence. However, this can cause misunderstandings, making them reserved and retiring. They cannot be demonstrative, and show their depth of feeling via their thoughtful acts of love and kindness.

They often find themselves the odd one out in a family.

Music helps them to unfold their deeply loving nature. It will be noticed from early years that they have a strong sense of money values and also the tendency to hoard things. When they are understood they make excellent friends and if genuinely encouraged, will try to give of their best. They strongly resent any interference, but if allowed to carry out small duties in their own way, they will help more often. To drive these children is to strengthen their defiance against you. This sets up a wall which takes years to penetrate. Parents who treat their number 8 children as friends generally have the most successful results. Many of these children suffer from loneliness even though they love the company of other children, and should be encouraged to mix with them if they appear stand-offish.

Number 8 children love nature and all beauty, particularly in music. They are happiest and most successful when helping others who are suffering or in trouble. These children love animals and should have some kind of pet to love and care for.

HARMONISING MONTHS FOR RULING NUMBER 8 PEOPLE

These months are the most powerful for major happenings in the life of a ruling 8 person: February (2), April (4), August (8).

SOME SUITABLE VOCATIONS FOR RULING NUMBER 8 PEOPLE

Heads of large businesses; senior executives; bankers; sharebrokers; travel agents; aircraft pilots; teachers; nurses to children/elderly; veterinary surgeons; working with animals; actors.

POSSIBLE HEALTH ISSUES FOR RULING NUMBER 8 PEOPLE
They are prone to problems with liver and bile, digestion and intestines. Also, congestion of the blood can bring on rheumatism.

Ruling number 9
The following are special characteristics of each combination of birthdate totals for ruling number 9 people.

9   These people would like to have responsibility and to do good charitable works, but they experience opposition.

18/9   They very often find themselves the focus of criticism. They desire independence but are not able to assert it.

27/9   They are often very restless, wish to travel and often do. They rarely show a desire to lead.

36/9   These are the people who organise communities and societies. They should be fortunate with contracts because of their psychic ability. They are inclined to worry about other people's troubles, which can have a negative impact on them.

45/9   They are inclined to scatter their forces and that does a lot of harm. On the other hand, they can become very helpful people, doing all kinds of good for humanity.

Number 9 is the highest mind number, the number of mystery. It is also said to embody the power of silence. It is the symbol that brings things to an end and prepares for new situations. It is a number of virtue, experience, morality, worthwhile rulership, human love, protection and the fruits of merit. It deals with art, particularly with literature and poetry, for it is a number of imagination and romance. Ruling number 9s are able to carry responsibility well; in fact, they are not happy unless they have responsibilities. These people always travel.

The number 9 has three times the strength of 3 and is a power that expresses fortune and misfortune — though what appears as misfortune to the world may not appear that way to a ruling number 9 person, as they have the wisdom of cosmic knowledge. To deal with humanity is the work of all 9s and they will never be happy until they recognise the unity of life and universal 'brotherhood of man'. They can do this more easily than most other vibrations. Their influence in a community is always felt and they attract more love than any other number because people feel their sympathy and their love, which they give freely. Ruling number 9 people are natural healers and carry a healing force with them. The number 9 is connected largely with literature and science and deals mainly with the deeper mental things of life.

These people are purely humanitarians, but must have freedom of thought. They have broad vision and are more fitted for wide principles and big plans than detail work.

They can help in international affairs, extending to all races, colours and creeds. They are very intuitive, just and honourable, having a strong inner desire to help and heal. When living up to the highest thought, they are messengers of progress and peace. Ordinary business is not for them. They give more than they take, and express themselves best through art or in helping humanity. They love to spend money, but rarely on themselves.

Ruling number 9 people need to be on the right path from an early age. They must guard against becoming opinionated or arrogant, and also against developing a desire for recognition and fame. 9 is the number of universal love and calls for tolerance, sympathy, individual expression, service and freedom.

People vibrating to this number usually occupy positions of trust and often have people working under them, so it brings responsibilities and care. It also attracts occupations that call for tact, diplomacy, good mental ability, good judgment and careful management. The number 9 is like energy that can never be destroyed. When 9 is multiplied by any other number it always reproduces itself.

POSITIVE NUMBER 9

These people are the humanitarians, the great dramatists, musicians, artists or orators, the universal lovers, the idealists who lead the people to God. They send out love and justice and mercy, seeking to make every person their friend — a prince or princess of earthly expression.

NEGATIVE NUMBER 9

These people can be the most dangerous of all vibrations when not properly guided and held in check against desire, falsehood and greed. They seek personal popularity and approval, could be home-breakers, breakers of hearts and faith, can be ruthless enemies, opinionated and touchy, seeing no side but their own.

RULING NUMBER 9 WOMEN

These women prefer to work for people rather than things. Many humanitarians are found among them and they will often take up outside interests, particularly for humanity. They are earnest whenever interested in a particular issue or subject. They make good friends, though they can be abrupt and apparently hard at times. Deep within, they are loving and anxious to please.

When number 9 women are true to themselves and doing what their hearts tell them, they have a strong sense of knowing and feeling for others. Many of them are called upon to sacrifice for others, so they must watch that they are not imposed upon. We look to the 9 woman for strength.

RULING NUMBER 9 MEN

If not engaged in humanitarian pursuits, these men are actors and can play the tragedian no matter what their calling may be. They need a strong companion to bring the best out in them or else they can grow careless in a general way. They can be sympathetic and charming at all times, especially at large gatherings.

They spend money freely, liking to make others happy, and will plan for what they feel would be best.

It is said that the 9 man in particular should be a rich man's son, perhaps because at heart he so much wants to give to others.

RULING NUMBER 9 CHILDREN

Children born under this vibration need careful training. They are loving and trusting, so be open and frank with them, otherwise they create a wall around themselves and become disinterested in the welfare of others. They are very sensitive and easily hurt; if misunderstood or mistreated by their parents, many of them run away from home.

They are stronger in spirit than physically and this inner strength drives them to dominate other children. They will need this inner strength in later years, but for now they must learn that their playmates might also like a turn at leadership.

The money instinct is very strong in these children and they should be brought up to respect money, to save and use it for special purposes. Some of these children will grow up to become financiers. If allowed to squander their money they lose all sense of values and soon become selfish spendthrifts. If parents teach that there is a big difference between their needs and their wants, it will help them to spend and save wisely.

They are sympathetic with anyone in trouble and suffering. They like responsibility, quickly losing interest if there is none. Music is essential in helping to unfold their deeper thinking: it is wisest for parents to expose their ruling 9 children to a range of harmonious music rather than to music that is discordant, thus helping them to establish positive thinking patterns early in life.

Regular habits are necessary for these children, otherwise they become careless and spend their energy needlessly.

HARMONISING MONTHS FOR RULING NUMBER 9 PEOPLE
These months are the most powerful for major happenings in the life of a ruling 9 person: March (3), June (6), September (9), December (12/3).

SOME SUITABLE VOCATIONS FOR RULING NUMBER 9 PEOPLE
Philosophers; scientists; composers; sculptors/artists/actors; preachers/ministers; surgeons; lawyers; working in charitable organisations; teachers.

POSSIBLE HEALTH ISSUES FOR RULING NUMBER 9 PEOPLE
These people spend their energy needlessly. Their reserve strength then fails them, and they worry. They are highly strung yet are able to control their feelings at the expense of their good health. Regular habits of every kind are necessary for good health.

Ruling number 10

The following are special characteristics of each combination of birthdate totals for ruling number 10 people.

10   These people will have a chance in life if they utilise strong initiative and have positive people around to help keep them confident.

19/10 They have the urge to assume responsibility and can only learn by taking it on, but they must guard against being imposed upon.

28/10 They are very often their own undoing, wearing out their reserves. When they are excessively energetic, they become stressed.

37/10 This is a very strong combination. The 3 and 7 are two psychic numbers that give power of expression in spiritual things, yet bring many trials, troubles and sorrows. However, if these tribulations are met, they will generate deep understanding.

46/10 These people are home-loving yet can be too forceful; then they find themselves alone. They must learn to see love in all things.

This is the number of leadership, originality and practical self-reliance. Ruling number 10 people are ambitious and strongly creative. They have willpower, confidence, determination of purpose and all the elements of success. This is a vibration of great courage and gives the ability to think and live independently.

10 is a powerful number, combining the unifying qualities of 1 with the mystical qualities of 0. Ruling number 10 people are the symbols of unity and individuality and represent perfection, harmony and order. Although they can be wilful, adaptability is the ruling trait of these people, both in general and in business. They often feel loneliness that they cannot describe but involvement with other people will help them overcome this.

These people adopt an air of debonair self-assurance and are generally accepted in any clothing that they choose to wear, regardless of the occasion. They are able to mix and to make themselves at home in any circumstances. They like antiques and curios and can be artistic.

They are usually artistic with a sensitive touch, making them competent instrumentalists and good judges of clothing and materials.

Ruling number 10 people are very adaptable and popular. They generally have a happy disposition that can become contagious. They do not delve deeply into life or other people's problems, and therefore find it difficult to understand why others are not as happy and as well adjusted as they are.

People vibrating to number 10 have the underlying principles of being creative, inventive, strongly individual, definite in their views and, in consequence, more or less obstinate and determined in all they undertake. It is primarily the vibration of the pioneer, the inventor, the leader, the explorer or anyone who aims at originality in any field. It indicates a strong nature in which lies the power to create, develop and govern all things pertaining to this life, but unlike the other numbers, it requires overcoming of self before attaining its highest success. These people dislike restraint. They are not easily rebuffed or drawn aside from their purpose and never acknowledge defeat. They are quick to recognise opportunities and grasp them strongly.

Ruling 10 people are not necessarily emotional but can be very staunch in their friendship. On the other hand, unless spiritually evolved, they can be bitter in enmity, inclined to be blunt and outspoken, and not always considerate of the effect of their words upon others. These people must guard against a tendency to dominate others.

They are capable of being the head of any enterprise, are good at buying and selling or as public lecturers or hosts. They are good managers, superintendents or in any capacity requiring original thought, ideas and management.

Many of them travel a lot as they grow older and this helps to settle their restless spirits. They are ambitious but must be trained very early to take responsibilities, otherwise they can drift away from their goals and the finer qualities are lost and their forces scattered.

POSITIVE NUMBER 10

These people are splendid creators of the original. They are independent thinkers and forge a path to higher living. Mostly, they are not stubborn or exalted in their own minds, but they can be high achievers with creative ability and intuition, courage, self-sufficiency and leadership qualities.

NEGATIVE NUMBER 10
These people can be conceited, dominant, arrogant, argumentative, critical and difficult to work with. This individual wants to do the thinking for everybody around them no matter how capable others are of solving their own problems.

This negative vibration could lead to intolerance, lack of appreciation of the fine qualities of others, nagging and repelling those with whom they come in contact.

RULING NUMBER 10 WOMEN
These women have a tendency to be abrupt and dominating. They can feel alone, especially when they do not fully understand their own emotions, and this can account for them having episodes of melancholia that can create misunderstandings.

Number 10 women are not particularly demonstrative and dislike any display of emotions. They are ambitious and can carry authority extremely well but those beneath them sometimes suffer. They are very fair, asking no more from life than they are prepared to give. They work hard at anything that interests them, and this is usually in the artistic world. It is not the height of their ambition to be domestic but if married they usually do all in their power to make the marriage successful. They are too practical to be romantic but can be valuable friends, wives and mothers. Usually in later life they are found in some type of public work as this helps to overcome any loneliness.

RULING NUMBER 10 MEN
These men resent being directed or influenced. They keep themselves separate and would rather work alone. They are not really happy if they have to work for a 'boss'.

They exude individuality and are meant to be leaders. The educated 10s become very efficient in everything they do. They like cheerful company but should learn to know that a certain amount of happiness needs to come from themselves; for a happy marriage, they need a very understanding partner. They are very fair to their children (more so than to their wives). They have a dictatorial tone of voice that upsets things at times. At heart they are kind, but the attitude 'I never bend' is always present.

RULING NUMBER 10 CHILDREN
Ruling number 10 children are very restless and always need to be busy. They crave outdoor interests and are never content if kept too closely within four walls. They have the spirit of adventure and parents do not easily understand this. If a certain amount of freedom is allowed, this will develop their nature. They like changes in the home and should be allowed to change their own possessions. They

love old things such as curios; also they appreciate good dress sense and artistic home surroundings.

If not properly understood, or if allowed to run wild, they become very selfish; otherwise they will help wherever they can. Parents are often surprised at the way these children bargain for things, even while very young, but they have the incentive to buy and sell, as this is really their field. They are also good at designing, interior decorating and creating original designs.

These children need plenty of rest. If they feel unwell and there appears to be no obvious cause, parents would be wise to consult a health professional.

HARMONISING MONTHS FOR RULING NUMBER 10 PEOPLE
These months are the most powerful for major happenings in the life of a ruling 10 person: May (5), October (10).

SOME SUITABLE VOCATIONS FOR RULING NUMBER 10 PEOPLE
Politicians; architects; business executives; real estate agents; interior decorators/designers; sales managers; writers; musicians; any occupation requiring original thought.

POSSIBLE HEALTH ISSUES FOR RULING NUMBER 10 PEOPLE
People who are born on the first of any month or whose ruling number is either 10 or 11, have a tendency to heart problems, caused through stress. Keeping calm, facing life

with faith and being positive can strengthen the cardiovascular system. If not dealt with, these heart issues can bring on high blood pressure in later life.

RULING NUMBER 11

The following are special characteristics of each combination of birthdate totals for ruling number 11 people.

11   These people can be sarcastic, mainly because they are frustrated. This may be because they experience difficulty in the way they voice their intuitive feelings.

29/11 These people are highly strung, often wishing to do more than they are able. They meet with much opposition, which causes misunderstanding. The more understanding the person, the more sensitive they are.

38/11 These people have good insight into things both material and spiritual, but they often have nervous troubles and headaches through misunderstandings.

47/11 This is a sacrificing number. These people would go without necessities to help others, so they must learn to be discerning. They are inclined to give unwisely of their own strength.

This is the number of spiritual guidance and from number 11 people we expect a message or word of comfort. This is their mission and if they accept and awaken to this gift they become the comfort of many.

They bring joy to their homes and loved ones. They are deep thinkers, honourable and willing to serve. Because their abilities are not in the material world, they find life difficult. They are not suited to hard-nosed business but will fit in where they feel it is necessary.

Ruling 11 people love refinement, beauty and culture. If they don't have these they become disinterested and find life difficult. They are positive people, strongly vibrant, impetuous, and inclined to be sarcastic at times, especially when opposed. They are idealists and dreamers and will introduce art in everything they do, even if it means conforming to material work.

If ruling number 11 people elevate themselves to the universal plane, it is said that all the forces for good conspire to help them. Within their souls they know the laws of the spiritual world as well as those of the material world. Many of them become spiritual teachers or missionaries.

11 is the symbol of genius. These people are inventors, originators, independent in action and thought, and in all cases stand for justice.

Awakened number 11 people are weighted with responsibility but are also able to feel the joy of living to the utmost. They delve deeply into the mystery of life and scarcely know when the 'seen' ends and the 'unseen' begins.

If these people are living on the material plane only, the number 11 indicates separation, unexpected happenings, the breaking up of existing conditions and a lack of good planning.

All ruling number 11 people must use their strong spiritual understanding in a constructive manner if they are to achieve real success. They can live with anyone but some of these people make unhappy marriages because they are deeply sensitive and can become extremely stressed.

POSITIVE NUMBER 11
These people are spiritual teachers. They are God's messengers to the human race, who constantly keep the message before them. They love refinement and beauty, are compassionate, honest and caring.

NEGATIVE NUMBER 11
These people are those who ignore faith and ideals. They will not teach or help others, but will antagonise everyone. They are domineering, cruelly critical and disparaging of others' work, morbidly sensitive and hold weak-minded superstitions.

RULING NUMBER 11 WOMEN
These women have high ideals and they build for the future. They are idealists, very decided in likes and dislikes, and do not easily fall in love. It is not in the nature of the number 11 woman to change in these ways. Many become spiritual teachers and missionaries. If not living constructively they can become selfish.

RULING NUMBER 11 MEN

These men are purely professional people, yet through difficult circumstances are often struggling to get through life. They understand spiritual philosophies that can guide them through their troubles, and if they give thought to these, it will really help them. Their happiest times are found in helping and guiding humanity.

They are very artistic, like good clothes and love their homes. The image of their mother and family is uppermost in their thoughts.

RULING NUMBER 11 CHILDREN

Ruling number 11 children are very highly strung. They are supersensitive and understand all that goes on around them. They have a tendency to worry very deeply if their family or people they love are in trouble. In fact, a lot of their illnesses are brought about through nerves.

If the home is peaceful these children gain a lot of strength, but if it is unhappy they will wish to run away. When they reach this stage they become sarcastic, critical and suspicious. This should never be allowed to happen, because these children are very loving, have a strong sense of right and wrong, and aim to be fair to all.

They will rise against any form of suppression and because of this, can fly into very bad tempers. Parents must realise that such children live on their nerves and must never be unjust or too hasty in meting out punishment.

These children will listen to reason and try to please. They are artistic, enjoy drawing and, as they mature, become interested in planning.

Ruling 11 children have high regard for home and family and are proud of them; they are ready to help whenever necessary. They love refinement, beauty and culture. If these children feel they are trusted, they will love and respect their parents.

HARMONISING MONTHS FOR RULING NUMBER 11 PEOPLE

These months are the most powerful for major happenings in the life of a ruling 11 person: April (4), July (7), November (11).

SOME SUITABLE VOCATIONS FOR RULING NUMBER 11 PEOPLE

Ministers/religious teachers; educators; writers; inventors; designers; artists; musicians. They are professional people who are suited to any following where they can express the revelation of truth and idealism.

POSSIBLE HEALTH ISSUES FOR RULING NUMBER 11 PEOPLE

People who are born on the first of any month or whose ruling number is either 10 or 11, have a tendency to heart problems, caused through stress. They are often described as nervy or highly strung. Keeping calm, facing life with faith and being positive can strengthen the nervous and cardiovascular systems. If not dealt with, these issues can bring on high blood pressure in later life.

RULING NUMBER 22/4

This number is spoken as 'twenty-two four'. When adding a birthdate, there is only one addition for this ruling number and that is 22. This is a master total; the double 2 gives great strength and also a spiritual mind. But if a person is also born on a 22 day, they find life very difficult and are equally hard to understand. They suffer a great deal.

The ruling number 22/4 is called a master number. There are two distinctly different types of ruling 22/4 people: the aware and the unaware. The aware 22/4s will be successful and master any aspect of life. The unaware 22/4s appear to be misfits and indifferent to life.

Ruling number 22/4 people have the ability to reach any height. They carry the combination of the spiritual and the material. They have the ability to build their dreams and ideas into reality. They are not easily understood, having complete control of their emotions, and this makes them appear indifferent and sometimes cold. In truth they are very sensitive and loving, but these feelings are deeply hidden and only love can bring forth their real nature. These people are the greatest philanthropists of all the ruling numbers. They are also lovers of art, rhythm, dancing and music.

22/4 people are wise, sympathetic and practical counsellors. With appropriate help and understanding they can choose their career and be sure of success. They can manage institutions successfully and their understanding helps them to qualify for the most difficult positions.

Ruling 22/4s are able to 'do' as well as 'talk'. The purpose of this vibration is to elevate the material to the plane of the spiritual. This number also attracts invention. It has been called an uncanny, remote, unearthly and intangible number. 22/4s either work too hard or not enough.

In marriage, few are really happy. They are strongly ambitious, which is not a road to lasting happiness. While their associates think them hard, cold and calculating, deep within their hearts they would like to be thought of as loving and kind.

POSITIVE NUMBER 22/4

These people are master builders in the world of form. They draw others to them for some great spiritual universal purpose, and fulfil expectations of those who believe in them. They are capable of being mystics, psychic or religious. They are calm, expressing power and poise and can hold great responsibility.

NEGATIVE NUMBER 22/4

These people are unreliable and indulgent. They sink into uselessness, are idle and build for themselves alone. They are full of fine schemes and great ideas, but are too unreliable or indolent to carry them out. They do nothing for the progress of the human race.

RULING NUMBER 22/4 WOMEN
The double vibration (material and spiritual) gives these women some of the vibrations of the ruling number 8 — independent and retiring. They can build, construct or create and express at will, although they are seldom demonstrative. If they keep the softness of the 2s, they are charming friends and kind to the helpless. They are efficient when constructive and like to be the heads and hearts of their families.

These women are not easy to know. They can appear so distant, yet they long for understanding. They have an attractive personality, particularly when in positions of power and leadership. They can become very lonely and it is best that they always keep interested. When happily married they are strong and are often mothers of statesmen and leaders.

RULING NUMBER 22/4 MEN
These are the master builders, the power salesmen and powerful thinkers. They attract by their personalities and make good through their efficiency. The 22/4 very often ends up with money. They are somewhat independent like the ruling number 8, and dislike working for others. If they do have to work for someone, they usually work their way quickly to the top. They seek happiness in or through other people but find that many people impose on their success and strength.

RULING NUMBER 22/4 CHILDREN

Children with the ruling number 22/4 are difficult to understand because they have complete control of their emotions. This is another powerful vibration with a combination of material and artistic abilities. If possible, attention should be paid to ensure these children have a good education.

Deep down they crave love and understanding and express their love in various acts of kindness. But parents must never expect these children to be demonstrative. They appear to be indifferent but this is a cover for their deep sensitivity. They can also be persistent and obstinately silent at times.

These children often cause heartaches for parents, especially if spoilt or neglected. To break a trust or misjudge them brings out the worst in their nature. If possible have them taught a musical instrument, as this is a great avenue of self-expression for these children and will make them easier to live with.

They can become exhausted and this disheartens them into feeling that they are failures. They need plain diet and plenty of relaxation. Once a friend, always a friend. Deep within there is a very real feeling of love and home.

They love beauty of rhythm and form and, as they grow older, they can qualify for the most difficult positions. This helps them to gain the happiness and peace they desire.

If 22/4 children make a mistake or do something wrong they are apparently unemotional and unmoved, seemingly having no regret or sorrow for their misdeed. Parents may feel that everything they say goes unheard and in vain and that they are meeting a barrier of coldness and indifference. But the opposite is true, because within themselves these 22/4 children are suffering deeply and feeling keenly everything around them.

Whatever parents might try to say, they can rest assured that these children are reasoning the problem in their own mind and that the strong inner power of these children should be met with patience and understanding, rather than resentment or frustration.

The following example will help to better understand ruling number 22/4 children and how to handle them. Suppose a 22/4 child left something out of place. If a parent said: 'Did you leave that thing there?' the child may not even reply and might persist in this obstinate silence, bringing the parent almost to breaking point. But if the parent had said: 'I wonder how this thing happened to get here?' the child would respond with a confession and explanation.

These children keenly resent any suggestion or accusation of their having done wrong; such situations bring out the worst in them.

HARMONISING MONTHS FOR RULING NUMBER 22/4 PEOPLE
These months are the most powerful for major happenings in the life of a ruling 22/4 person: February (2), April (4), August (8).

SOME SUITABLE VOCATIONS FOR RULING NUMBER 22/4 PEOPLE

IT field; politics; humanitarians; philanthropists; teachers; any of the arts; can qualify to hold the most difficult positions and to manage institutions successfully.

POSSIBLE HEALTH ISSUES FOR RULING NUMBER 22/4 PEOPLE

Like ruling 4 people, ruling 22/4s suffer with ailments that are sometimes difficult to describe. They are inclined to melancholia and a very discontented mind, which can result in headaches, kidney, liver and bladder troubles. They are often not very strong physically.

RULING NUMBER 33/6

When I first wrote *Numerology, Numbers and their Influence* I did not add the now much talked about Master Number 33/6. There was no mention of it being a Master Number in my Grandmother Hettie Templeton's published books on Numerology in 1940 and 1956. And indeed, prior to those years and during that era there was no strong talk of it at all. The only master numbers seriously spoken of at that time were the 11 and the 22.

During the 1960s Hettie Templeton mentioned to me that the 33 had a strong and unusual energy but still had not considered it a master number, and as she was my teacher I submitted to her thought.

Now, in the 21st century, because of the growing consideration of the 33 as a master number, I decided to do my own research and have met and spoken with several ruling number 33/6 people. Four are friends and a fifth, a dear nephew.

There are basic similarities with all ruling numbers, no matter what the addition (e.g. 2+4=6; 3+3=6; 2+3=5; 3+2=5; 2+1=3; 3+0=3; etcetera.) I have discovered that every ruling number separates from basic similarities after an indefinable point, where the person's capabilities become more definable. Once these qualities are revealed we begin to see people as individuals. The deeper the birthday numbers are investigated the more they reveal themselves.

Here I now add the 33 to the master numbers 11 and 22.

All 33/6s have a vibrant, bright energy field. Upon their shoulders is placed great responsibility and they have a deep inner knowledge of this. No matter which vocation they choose, inspiration will always be the apex of their message.

The 33 is, above all, the Inspirational Master Teacher.

Their energies are different and unusual, and like most master numbers these people probably wonder where in life they fit in. This is one reason why some never rise above that indefinable point mentioned above. It is at this time that the 33/6 person becomes more like the basic ruling No. 6. They do not have the deeper understanding of what their particular number, 33/6, requires of them and consequently often go through life feeling confused. This happens because they need to find the balance between the energy and knowledge that comes from deep within them. Some might consider it that spark of intelligence from the 'higher realms'; that mystical place that delivers our spark of genius. Indeed, from where do any of us receive that spark of genius?

It is because most master numbers do not have this understanding of themselves that confusion steps in and many then turn to negativity. But once this understanding is realised the chance of having [more] balance in their lives becomes a reality.

There are those among the master numbers who realise – perhaps from an early age – that they have a certain inner strength or quality that gives them the incentive to push onwards.

The 33/6 looks for perfection in everybody and everything and if in their eyes a person or thing does not line up to that perfection, their 'perception' often causes them to talk and think negatively. This appears to affect the balance of their thought processes.

However, when it can be explained to them that there is no such thing in our reality as a perfect person or thing, it changes their thinking and therefore changes their lives, leading them in a positive direction.

Self doubt and negativity appear to be the biggest hurdles in their lives – and it's this combination that sends their emotions swinging between states of over-confidence and deep negative doubt.

Their whole outlook becomes more positive once they realise their high ideals are given to them to create inspiration when teaching or speaking, and not something with which to evaluate the world they see around them.

All 33/6s tend to hide their real emotions and to remain cool and calm on the surface, but this does not help their close relationships. It would help immensely if they learned to express their real feelings; to be more open; and try to be natural and have people accept them as they really are. This would also help in calming their nerves, as all ruling 6s suffer with nerve problems.

33/6s might give thought to using a step-by-step method when aiming for a goal. Often what happens is they 'see' the project completed and have this urgency to achieve it quickly without being practical; this is not advantageous [to them.]

These people are capable of making a success of almost any vocation they choose – especially if they learn to keep that naughty word 'doubt' out of the equation. They are generally professional types and can be wonderful communicators and writers. They also like to make sure that the spiritual needs of others are met.

It is interesting to note that the spine has 33 segments. As the Kundalini rises it opens the chakras causing a tingling sensation, which is indicative of the Kundalini energising and awakening these areas.

Also interesting is that certain words add to 33 – the word Diamond being one. A man usually gives his girl a diamond to show his love when he asks for her hand in marriage.

Author Stuart Wilde named one of his books *Infinite Self – 33 Steps to Reclaiming Your Inner Power.*

The word Teacher also adds to 33.

When 33/6 people learn to show their full worth and not be afraid to express themselves, their lives will change, bringing them happiness – especially when they remember that, above all, they are the Master Teachers, who are themselves inspired to put inspiration into the hearts of others.

POSITIVE NUMBER 33/6

There is an aura of vibrant energy and understanding around these people. They are visibly positive and nurturing types and will often talk with inspiration, building hope and looking to the future. Their bright moving energy seems to 'rub off' onto the 'listener.'

NEGATIVE NUMBER 33/6

When a 33/6 person is afraid to move forward, they become negative. They know that deep within there is something more in them but they don't take that forward step, allowing doubt to step in. This leads to them being 'nosey' and to occasionally not mind their own business. They will talk with a negative outcome, perhaps giving unwanted advice. There will be times when the light of positivity shines through and one might get the feeling that there is something more within these folk.

RULING NUMBER 33/6 WOMEN

All Ruling 6s including 33/6s like food and like to cook. They are capable of being in charge of pastry shops or head large restaurants or food organisations. The women are extremely nurturing and can aspire to medicine or a vocation along those lines. If doubt steps in to hold them back they must learn to be positive, knowing that 'they can do it.' In fact, all types of vocations are open to them. Under most circumstances, in any vocation, a student would be extremely fortunate to have a 33/6 for a teacher.

RULING NUMBER 33/6 MEN
If these people have the desire to achieve in an academic world they will shine. Some might prefer to write or to inspire whilst philosophising. Doubt is always their enemy – but with strong positive energy these people can follow their own ideas and be successful in any vocation.

RULING NUMBER 33/6 CHILDREN
One of the most noticeable aspects of these little folk is that they love to laugh and be happy most of the time. They are very loving and show it in the hugs they like to give and receive, and performing small tasks for members of their family, whom they love. This act brings joy to the child.

There is a joyous, vibrant energy about them. When they are unhappy or sad, that energy of 'light' around them dims – something that an observant parent will recognise immediately. This is the time to tell the child they are very much loved and to give them a warm hug. At this point the child might tell the parent about a problem he/she has, and might like to talk it over. There's an old saying: 'Out of the mouths of babes ...' and it is the wise parent who gives some time to listen to what these little ones have to say at certain important moments in the child's life.

During play, the 33/6 child might often be explaining particular things to a small group of other children – as in being the teacher, or showing them how something works.

These children are quite nervy and often become fretful. If this happens, endeavour to get to the cause of the problem.

Further reading can be obtained on the number 6 child on page 44 in this book.

HARMONISING MONTHS FOR ALL RULING NUMBER 6 PEOPLE

See page 45 as this is the same for all Ruling Number 6 people.

SOME SUITABLE VOCATIONS FOR 33/6 PEOPLE

Most Fields of Medicine; Healing; Teaching; Forms of Humanitarianism; Charitable Organisations; Education; Politics; Ministers of the Church; Directors of large Organisations; in fact anything they choose because their true desire is to inspire no matter what their vocation – and there is a long list. These folk will go above and beyond the call of duty.

POSSIBLE HEALTH ISSUES FOR RULING NUMBER 33/6 PEOPLE

All Ruling 6 people suffer from nervous disorders in varying degrees. There is often irregular circulation of the blood, which affects the heart.

Worry is mainly responsible for their many ailments. All types of 6s must learn to concentrate. This helps with focus, good health and peace of mind, otherwise their energies become scattered, leading to a restless soul.

DAY NUMBERS

An individual's day number derives from the date of the day on which that person is born, and unlike the ruling number, can be a number 1.

Our day number is often said to reveal 'the other side' of us. In the Pythagorean method it certainly does play a part in our lives, but should never take precedence over our ruling number: if we are living through the vibrations of our day number, we are not living our true life pathway.

Since the day number will generally be different from the ruling number and can sometimes be a stronger vibration, we need to be fully aware of this and live mindfully, choosing a life path that resonates with our ruling number vibration. Consider the example of a person who has a day number of 22/4. Their ruling number will generally be anything from 2 to 11. Since 22/4 is such a powerful day number, this person may be drawn strongly to live the pathway of 22/4 rather than living according to the vibration of their ruling number.

If both the ruling number and the day number are odd, the person will have a dynamic personality; some may even tend towards aggression. When both ruling number and day number are even, the person will not be particularly demonstrative and will have a placid temperament.

When someone has the same day number as their ruling number, the vibration of that number tends to be emphasised. This individual does not have that 'other side' to explore to such a great extent. People who have 22/4 both as day number and ruling number are likely to have difficult lives.

To avoid misunderstandings on how the day numbers are calculated, all day numbers are listed here:

DATE BORN	DAY NUMBER
first day of the month	1
second day of the month	2
third day of the month	3
fourth day of the month	4
fifth day of the month	5
sixth day of the month	6
seventh day of the month	7
eighth day of the month	8
ninth day of the month	9
10th day of the month	10
11th day of the month	11
12th day of the month	3
13th day of the month	4
14th day of the month	5

15th day of the month	6
16th day of the month	7
17th day of the month	8
18th day of the month	9
19th day of the month	10
20th day of the month	2
21st day of the month	3
22nd day of the month	22/4
23rd day of the month	5
24th day of the month	6
25th day of the month	7
26th day of the month	8
27th day of the month	9
28th day of the month	10
29th day of the month	11
30th day of the month	3
31st day of the month	4

THE MEANINGS OF THE DAY NUMBERS

The day number will have similar aspects to the ruling number. But, as already stated, the ruling number must be regarded as the true number of the life path; otherwise life's dreams may ultimately fall away.

DAY NUMBER 1

These people yearn to work alone. They feel compact within themselves and shine when permitted to work independently and to be alone part of the time. They can feel complete within themselves and because of this, may tend not to live on the side of their ruling number. They must look to their ruling number for direction. Their influencing planet is the Sun, which brings strength. This is also the number of individualism.

DAY NUMBER 2
This is a number of intuition, which is valuable when making decisions. These people like to be around and work with happy people, and are reliable as well as supportive.

DAY NUMBER 3
These people love humour in all its forms, and usually have an active brain, making them quick thinkers. There are times when they have the urge to criticise, which should be avoided. It would not be unusual for any of these people to be found among the art/music/creative world. Some will have religion or spirituality in their lives, and might have well developed psychic abilities.

DAY NUMBER 4
These people have good organisational skills, are practical and capable. Those who have an odd ruling number can follow in the direction of that number, knowing their material wellbeing is supported. If their ruling number is even, they need to avoid emphasis on materialism. These people have a natural talent to plan, work and build.

DAY NUMBER 5

These people have good communication skills. They may also have the ability to write and perhaps work as journalists, depending on their ruling number. The number 5 always means love of freedom, change and travel. Like those with the ruling number 5, day number 5 people must watch that they do not make promises and lightly break them.

DAY NUMBER 6

These people may be restricted to domestic activities. They prefer harmony, love and beauty in the home. They must guard against over-worrying, anxiety and complaining. Engaging in a hobby helps them establish and maintain a positive focus rather than complaining. They are otherwise very loving people.

DAY NUMBER 7

These people learn the lessons of life by personal sacrifice. This can often affect love, health or the pocket — very often the sacrifice will be felt most readily in the pocket. As they grow older and life's lessons have been thoroughly instilled, they may be drawn to the public in some way. These people will then have deep understanding and will delve into the meaning of life in some small or large way.

DAY NUMBER 8

Personal independence is the nature of this day number. Many of these people may believe that this number will provide them with financial independence and they will work towards this, rather than recognising this number as independence of the self. As these people mature their financial success will be based on the understanding on how they live their lives.

DAY NUMBER 9
Many people with this day number appear quite serious and tend to become too ambitious. This is a number that stands for universal love and these people should direct their ambitions towards the common good. They must avoid arguments because their seriousness gives the impression of being dictatorial.

DAY NUMBER 10
These people are generous and energetic: the number 10 is known for its adaptability. They have the ability to lead and won't hesitate to grasp an opportunity when they see it.

DAY NUMBER 11
This is the number of spirituality and intuition. From time to time these people may live in emotional extremes. When this happens it exhibits as moodiness and should be controlled for the sake of good health. There are times when these people would be well advised to think before they speak. This may happen when intuition comes through strongly and they fumble their words while trying to express their insights.

DAY NUMBER 22/4

Anything is possible with this number and these people can reach any goal. But they should realise that for them, 22/4 is a day number influence and not a ruling number influence. 22/4 is a powerful aspect and there is a good chance that people with this day number will gravitate towards it rather than living by their ruling number. If this happens, they are likely to live an 'unbalanced' life where their dreams are shattered. They are urged to read carefully about their ruling number and be guided by it, knowing that they have a strong back-up in their day number.

LOVE INTERESTS/PARTNERSHIPS FOR EACH RULING NUMBER

RULING NO.2

These people love to be romanced. Planning a romantic evening every so often with lots of thought will go a long way towards making them feel special – and don't forget to show your co-operative side when it's needed. These folk are usually of the gentle type.

RULING NO.3

When your partner is a 3 ruling number, always keep in mind that they appreciate laughter and light-heartedness. You might not always feel this way yourself, but keep it in mind and do your best to show your appreciation for who they are. This understanding attitude will certainly reap rewards. On the other hand, discussion always helps.

RULING NO.4
Keep conversation or explanations clear and precise so that your number 4 partner can chronologically understand you perfectly. This way any misunderstandings will be kept to a minimum and your partner will appreciate it, and you, immensely.

RULING NO.5
Show interest in what your number 5 partner is interested in, but do not over-crowd him/her. Adventure and change are their keywords. Keep this in mind and your partner will not be bored. Being bored or restless for them is their own personal nightmare. They will love being surprised.

RULING NO.6
This partner will always expect you to be there for them. Show appreciation when and where necessary. Speak your love occasionally – and a little gift wouldn't go astray. Keep in mind they have deep love for their family.

RULING NO.7
This partnership could be tricky because 7s are seemingly a law unto themselves. The advice here would be to take note of their moods; talk things over when necessary and

bring balance into the relationship, remembering that a partnership is a two-way street.

RULING NO.8
These people do not like to be told, unless they ask. Do not 'hover' over or around them. When they speak their mind strongly, digest what they say and how they've said it before 'jumping in'. You will discover that their nature is usually very loving.

RULING NO.9
If you remember that 9s love to love everybody including animals, it will help you to see them with more compassion. Occasionally ask how they are feeling and perhaps offer to do something for them, instead of them doing for you. They in turn will see you in a better light.

RULING NO.10
These people are usually fairly independent as partners. They don't like being questioned because they feel that they rule the roost. If they are permitted to have their own way occasionally instead of you fighting it, there will be deep appreciation and caring on their part.

RULING NO.11
They are deep thinkers so sometimes you might find them in another world, with you having to repeat your question etcetera. As their partner, try to understand this. Perhaps

they might like to talk about it. They love beauty and refinement in all things, so a little TLC over a candlelit dinner might do the trick to help a situation.

RULING NO. 22/4
These people can be somewhat like the ruling 4, only more pronounced. They will either feel successful or feel like a misfit. Either way, do your best to show that they are important to you.

RULING NO.33/6
In this partnership the advice is to listen to what these people have to say in certain situations because somewhere in their words could be 'the key' to understanding them on a deeper level. This ultimately leads to much appreciation and love between you both.

PERSONAL YEAR NUMBERS

While some aspects of an individual's numerology are unchangeable, other aspects move through cycles or can be changed. The aspects that remain fixed are the ruling number, the day number, the birthdate chart and the ages at which the pyramid peaks (see Chapter 6) occur on an individual's chart.

For each individual, personal year numbers rotate through a nine-year cycle. (The influential pyramid peak numbers also change each nine years within a 27-year cycle.) A person can also influence their own or their child's vibration with the name they choose, are given or use, but it is worth remembering that a name change takes from three to six months for the vibrations to be influential.

Personal year numbers, governed by the actual year in which the calculation is being done, distil down to the numbers 2 (can sometimes be 11), 3, 4 (can sometimes be 22/4), 5, 6, 7, 8, 9 and 10.

We each have our own vibrations, and if we live with other people there will be plenty of opportunities for both harmony and discord. Take the example of a couple living together. One partner may be under a dynamic personal year number; the other partner may be under a much less dynamic personal year number. Under such circumstances, these partners can live most harmoniously by understanding and helping each other, giving moral support and strength.

Since some people react strongly to change, after experiencing a year or more of positive aspects where things tend to go well, it can be difficult for them to adjust to lower vibrations which may bring some negative aspects.

Knowing our personal year numbers helps us to understand what type of year to expect so that we can be ready to accept what comes and work with it. Sometimes this takes courage. It is when we resist that things tend to go wrong. We must learn to co-operate with the prevailing vibrations if we want our lives to run more smoothly.

CALCULATING PERSONAL YEAR NUMBERS (PYNS)

Add the number/s of the **day of birth** to those of the **month of birth** and then add the **current year number** (note that the year of birth is **not** involved in PYN calculations). For the year 2006 (2 + 6 = 8), for example, the current year number is 8.

Here are some examples of personal year number calculations for different birthdates.

BIRTHDATE EXAMPLE

15 August 1974 in the year 2006

Add 1 + 5 + 8 + 8 = 22.

Then add 2 + 2 = 4.

The final number is 22/4 (do not reduce this number).

So, a person born on 15 August (in any year) would be under the vibrations of a PYN of 22/4 in the year 2006.

BIRTHDATE EXAMPLE

18 September 1945 in the year 2006

Add 1 + 8 + 9 + 8 = 26 (reduce this number).

Add 2 + 6 = 8.

So, the person born on 18 September (in any year) would be under the vibrations of a PYN of 8 in the year 2006.

In the year 2007 (2 + 0 + 0 + 7 = 9) the current year number would be 9.

BIRTHDATE EXAMPLE

29 September 1940 in the year 2007

Add 2 + 9 + 9 + 9 = 29 (reduce this number).

Add 2 + 9 = 11 (do not reduce this number).

So, the person born on 29 September (in any year) would be under the vibrations of a PYN 11 in the year of 2007.

In the year 2011 (2 + 0 + 1 + 1 = 4) the current year number would be 4.

BIRTHDATE EXAMPLE

1 November 1938 in the year 2011.

Add 1 + 1 + 1 + 4 = 7.

So, the person born on 1 November (in any year) would be under the vibrations of a PYN 7 in the year 2011.

THE MEANINGS OF THE PERSONAL YEAR NUMBERS

To gain the greatest understanding from looking at your personal year number, consider it in context with your ruling number and pyramid peak numbers (see Chapter 6 on pyramids and Chapter 7 for detailed examples of applying PYN insights to decision making). If you are on your pyramids, look at whether you are rising to the peak, on the peak, coming off the peak or somewhere in the middle (between peaks). For example, the period between peaks, say in a personal year 4 or 5, is usually a relatively dormant period. A PYN 6 is sometimes referred to as a mini-peak during which all sorts of things can come to fruition.

PERSONAL YEAR NUMBER 2

This vibration has the tendency to bring things to a standstill. There may be new opportunities arising but they will not generally be of a powerful nature, although they may be helpful in some way. In this quieter period, there is opportunity to study or to build on what you already have. This vibration can be a sensitive one and there may be a few personal heartaches. Endeavour to have pleasant, happy company around you.

The best way to handle the energies this year is to be co-operative, considerate and friendly, especially in the face of adversity. Do your best not to be impulsive.

Be mindful and understanding with any type of relationships. If you are working in the positive there could be new types of relationships on the horizon.

If there are any working plans underway in the mix please be patient and wait for them to come to fruition.

Ruling number 2 people in a PYN 2 need to take great care to maintain their health, and may experience disappointment in somebody or something.

PERSONAL YEAR NUMBER 3

This can be a happy year. It is a time when new friends emerge to be added to the circle of older friends. This vibration is generally thought of as bright and happy.

Do not become overexcited and do something impulsive like overspend.

Remember that old adage: 'You can catch more flies with honey than you can with vinegar'? Well then, do your best and use more honey this year and less vinegar.

In a 3 personal year do not look for rewards without putting in effort.

Invitations will come your way. Go out, entertain, have fun, but be careful not to overtax the nervous system. You may have the opportunity to go on short journeys.

Don't be too quick in making decisions because it is easy to make a change at the wrong time under this happy aspect.

This vibration often brings some kind of sorrow or illness to someone you know.

Ruling number 3 people in a PYN 3 will be inclined to scatter their nervous energy.

PERSONAL YEAR NUMBER 4

This is a practical year and it can be a rather trying time. While this can be a year to lay a foundation for security, it is also a year of frustrations with setbacks and opposition. However, if you are prudent, there could be an opportunity to buy or sell this year. It is also a year to put any ideas you might have into concrete form. Under this type of year there is rarely time for personal pleasures. Responsibility involving work will increase, but so will your ability to organise.

While under this aspect, watch your diet carefully and be careful of your health. It would be beneficial to rest when you can and perhaps lighten your workload. Perhaps towards the end of the year you might take several days away to recuperate.

Be satisfied to bide your time and wait for April to pass, then begin anything new between May and August.

Watch your spending habits under this aspect because you could 'save pennies and spend pounds'.

Tidy up your affairs to make way for your next busy year.

Ruling number 4 people in a PYN 4 may experience limitations and a feeling that life is nothing but work.

PERSONAL YEAR NUMBER 5

Last year (personal year number 4) was one of work and organisation. This year certainly makes up for it. It is a year of personal freedom — being able to express yourself the way you want to. There are new opportunities and friends, holidays, change and variety. Learn something new but don't take on too much or you may scatter your forces. Under this aspect, learn to prioritise and delegate. This vibration often starts the need to learn, or perhaps take an art or other creative course, particularly if your ruling number is 5 or 10.

Keep in mind that under the 5 aspect there will always be the unexpected; and it could be a positive or a negative. Ideas might come that you could put into place next year. This should be a year of progress and freedom.

Ruling number 5 people in a PYN 5 need to guard against the tendency to misuse their feelings of freedom, and are at risk of being careless and making mistakes.

PERSONAL YEAR NUMBER 6

This year brings responsibilities, especially in connection with home life. You may be looking to buy or sell, or to renovate. If renting, you may change your address or rearrange your home furnishings.

This is a romantic number. It is a friendly influence for new friendships, love, engagements, marriage and babies.

On the other hand, there are those who decide to separate simply because they meet a new attraction, which rarely lasts. So many couples make sad mistakes under this influence. But there are also many happy reconciliations.

If there is anything to be discussed this year, now is the time to bring it into the open and talk about it. Please be mindful that we cannot always expect people or situations to be just as we might like them to be – you are not the only one in the conversation. There might be other people or issues to be considered.

Businesses can flourish under this aspect. Big companies are formed and business people under this influence often receive wonderful opportunities, which in turn can strengthen the home front.

Ruling number 6 people in a PYN 6 are likely to experience excessive responsibility at home.

PERSONAL YEAR NUMBER 7

Some dread the 7 in many ways. Certainly, it is the number of sacrifice but when it comes as an aspect it is not to be feared. This is a year to consolidate.

It would be of enormous help to you this year to be understanding in the face of adversity. Do your best not to force issues. Use a gentle approach and your reward could be 'positives' later in the year.

Nothing in a business way should be started, nor is it a time to sell.

The urge to teach and write often begins under this influence and if followed would be successful. This year is referred to as a time for mental cleansing: where the 4 lays the foundation for security, the 7 lays the foundation for inner strength and power. From this year may emerge a goal and a plan of great importance.

This would be a good time to study if the opportunity arose.

Ruling number 7 people in a PYN 7 are unlikely to experience any opportunities for material advancement.

PERSONAL YEAR NUMBER 8

This is a year for personal change and progress in business. Under this influence you may plan to buy or sell.

This year will be a firm taskmaster (ruled by the planet Saturn), so be sure all dealings are straight and honest because you could be exposed while under this aspect.

If you are just and ethical in all things, success will be assured. But never underestimate those with whom you are dealing.

Speculations in various ways will open up opportunities. This influence gives courage, which it is wise to utilise. Many people reap rewards under this vibration, especially after years of sacrifice.

This is a year of restlessness. Perhaps you're thinking of a change of job or to make some other change. This is a high energy year so be ready for what is to come.

Make sure you are thoughtful and kind to others throughout the year. You must learn not to fight against any minor adversities. Rather go with the flow and learn to work through them. You will discover more happiness this way and the year will be easier.

The number 8 is the power of balance and levelling. For those who fall short, loss will be experienced.

Ruling number 8 people in a PYN 8 are likely to be challenged by physical and material strain.

PERSONAL YEAR NUMBER 9

This is a very exacting vibration. It means the ending of many things that have weighed heavily, and presents the opportunity for new beginnings. This is a time to stop and think. In fact, it demands a new beginning.

This influence will often mean the parting of friends and business partners or the ending of a job, but there is always the opportunity for something better.

If there is someone or something in your life, for which you have no further use and you are still hanging on, this might be the time to let go. It serves no purpose hanging on.

Express feelings of love to everybody, settle any old scores and forgive where necessary. Reward is then at hand.

Ruling number 9 people in a PYN 9 will be particularly impacted by emotional strain and sacrifice of some kind, and should watch their health during this period.

PERSONAL YEAR NUMBER 10

This aspect often brings big changes, often a complete change in the way of thinking. There is a tendency to lose interest in some things and a strong feeling to stand alone and to make your own decisions. If those decisions are of a conservative nature they will be successful. Once the unsettled feeling passes then you will reap the benefit of changes made in the previous year.

It must be understood that to benefit from favourable changes and success we must live unselfishly. Many people expect a lot without much effort; then, when things go wrong, they lose heart.

Don't be afraid to put forward any new project you might have in mind. Take it easy and don't be impulsive. If you are 'on the ball' you should recognise an opportunity during the year.

Ruling number 10 people in a PYN 10 will often experience extreme unrest, may be disagreeable, and might even appear momentarily to be 'losing the plot'.

PERSONAL YEAR NUMBER 11

There will be some times during a lifetime when the personal year number totals an 11 rather than a 2. Some people, such as those born on, say, 29/9 will never experience a PYN 2, but always an 11 following on from the PYN 10. This is because the 29 and the 9 already add to 20; when the current year is added to this, the result will always be higher than 20. Hence, it can never reduce to a PYN 2.

The person under a PYN 11 will feel extra sensitive and nervy, which creates misunderstandings with friends and family. Spiritual ideals rather than a materialistic attitude should be the goal during this year, so that its influence enhances the power to motivate others.

Be considerate, friendly and patient and allow any plans made last year to come to fruition. Try not to be impulsive.

This is a year somewhat like the 7. It is a good time to learn and expand inner knowledge.

There is often the desire to make changes but it is never wise to rush things under an 11 vibration, unless absolutely necessary.

Many children under this number find it hard to concentrate, so support, encouragement and consideration are necessary.

Ruling number 11 people in a PYN 11 may find this an exceptionally stressful year that impacts negatively on the brain and their thought processes.

PERSONAL YEAR NUMBER 22/4

This is a strong influence, one where successful opportunities arise.

Under this influence, many people may begin something that will help humankind. Others will write or begin to plan unselfish deeds for others.

This year could bring responsibility on your shoulders. It is a time to put projects and ideas into concrete form. Work hard and diligently and your rewards will come. Do not be careless with your finances, but use your common sense.

Those who live selfishly may find this vibration a destructive force, creating an indifferent feeling in general.

The influence of the 22/4 personal year number will be stronger than the personal year number 4.

This can be a strong year, so make good use of it.

The health must be carefully watched.

Ruling number 22/4 people in a PYN 22/4 may be dealt a nasty shock on a personal level.

PERSONAL YEAR NUMBER 33/6

Basically, number 6 personal year vibrations are similar, but when a person comes under the 33/6 personal year vibration, they have the ability and the capacity to go further and deeper than any other type of 6, and that's one reason why 33/6 is called a Master Number.

So, whilst the normal basic meaning of the number 6 personal year applies here, the 33/6 personal year has the capacity for the person to give more of themselves and perhaps take certain issues in the year to a deeper level.

(Read about the number 6 personal year number on pages 41-45)

The 33/6 is a year when you might give your services to others and, where possible, forget the Self for the time being. It could come to pass that there are people around you who need your help, either by using your inspiring words or your healing hands; and if so, you might decide to give your help in either or both directions.

Remember one of your main aims in a 33/6 year is to be an inspiration to others. So always give of your best in this wonderful year of opportunity, where you might well make a difference in someone's life.

Because your responsibilities are bound to be heavy this year, you must not over-tax your own energies. Give yourself some consideration and rest when necessary.

Also, for your own well-being do your best to mix with happy people and have some happy times. This helps to remove some of the heaviness that this year has placed upon you.

A few examples of a 33/6 Ruling Number birthday:

4th August, 1956 = 33/6   (4+8+1+9+5+6 = 33)

29th January, 1965 = 33/6   (2+9+1+1+9+6+5 = 33)

14th July, 1974 = 33/6   (1+4+7+1+9+7+4 = 33)

2nd April, 1989 = 33/6   (2+4+1+9+8+9 = 33)

4th June, 1994 = 33/6   (4+6+1+9+9+4 = 33)

11, 22 AND 33 COMBINED WITH OTHER NUMBERS

The reader is asked to note that while the 11 and 22 can occur as both a day number or a ruling number, the 33 can of course only occur as a ruling number.

As we have already seen, the numbers 11, 22 and 33 have special qualities. They are generally known as master numbers. People who have 11 and 22 as their day or ruling number, or 33 as their ruling number must awaken to a realisation of the 11, 22 and 33 in order to activate these qualities in their lives.

The 11 is a spiritually inspired number with the potential for genius. The 22 is double 11 — highly spiritual energy resting over the practical number of 4 (22/4) — and is known as the master builder. Number 33 is known as the master teacher.

Number 11 people must balance their inspirational / psychic gift with the skills required for living in the practical world. While it often seems simpler for them to drift towards the comforts of practical living, rather than heeding the inner / prophetic voice they are blessed with, this choice will result in a deep unhappiness. When they learn to balance their spiritual gift with the practicalities of everyday living, they will achieve happiness.

22/4 people can find it even more difficult than 11 people to establish balance in their lives. Unfortunately, many live either in the world of inspiration only, or choose a lifestyle focused on instant gratification. The unenlightened 22/4 is often confused, not knowing which world they belong to. But when they become aware that their lives must be balanced between the spiritual and the practical, they discover they can live in both worlds. Then, they have the capacity to become the most successful of all the numbers, in any field of endeavour they choose. Because of their special powers, when 11, 22 and 33 are combined with other numbers they impact on them as well. This occurs for all people whose ruling or day number is an 11 or 22, or their ruling number is 33.

Because of their special powers, when 11 and 22 are combined with other numbers, they impact on them as well. This occurs for all people whose ruling or day number is an 11 or a 22.

Here is a summary of the potential they have with each of the other numbers:

11 — 1/10   A psychic adept.

22 — 1/10   A master adept; a seer and a psychic. This person is likely to deal with spiritual things and their manifestations.

33 — 1/10   These people have vision and can reach great achievement in most areas.

11 — 2   A seer and a psychic. This person will deal with spiritual things and their manifestations.

22 — 2   A master seer, and a collector of mental and physical things.

33 — 2 People who can aspire to become wonderful counsellors in the field of mental health.

11 — 3 People who will see deeply beneath the surface of nature and are inclined to be involved in science or religion.

22 — 3 A master adept and seer dealing with all of nature's forces, music, art and scientific inventions.

33 — 3 They will have brilliant ideas but must keep the mind focussed to achieve the success they desire. Giving talks and doing some writing should have a pleasant outcome.

11 — 4 These people try to harmonise religion and science. They can be active workers in an evangelical capacity.

22 — 4 Wise about books and eduction, these people can make a success of buying for stores or for themselves. They tend to be athletic.

33 — 4 These people have the ability to achieve in the architectural profession and in the building trade. They have the vision to see the completed works.

11 — 5 They see and know many things about other people, but often fail to take note of these insights. They have fine, active minds.

22 — 5 These people have versatile intellects and can write expressively on any topic. They are charming, and love to be up-to-date on what is happening in the world. People with this influence often do well in magazine journalism.

33 — 5   They make great inventors and have marvellous creative/artistic skills. They possess a beautiful flowing energy.

11 — 6   This combination can achieve harmonious balance. They make good teachers and preachers, and are also good at making money.

22 — 6   These people know and understand much more about the unseen forces of nature than they can express. They are the masters of the material forces of nature and are excellent money makers.

33 — 6   There is a possibility of some conflict within them. They might consider endeavouring to keep focussed and listening to their inner voice for inspiration, and then success is theirs.

11 — 7   These mystical people are fitted for any profession, as they encompass all of creation with the breadth and depth of their thought.

22 — 7   The master minds of real estate, these people are also good writers and teachers of the occult truth.

33 — 7   These people might dream of worlds beyond our own. They have the ability to achieve in any field of Science. They might like to acquire editing skills if that be their desire.

11 — 8   This is a proud vibration. Such people may be tempted to lose contact with their sympathetic or compassionate aspect if they become intensely involved in something they believe to be important.

22 — 8 They extend beyond the limits of expression, seeing and feeling like the master mystics that they are.

33 — 8 They have great ability to lead in the corporate world or be brilliant in the Stock Exchange. They also might aspire to become involved in veterinary science.

11 — 9 These people would be welcomed upon the platform of any congressional hall or in any place where great human interests are at stake. They also write well on world topics.

22 — 9 With their capacity to be masters of universal law and love, these people need to know how to deal with other people and their interests.

33 — 9 These people have the ability to shine as humanitarians and possibly run a charity organisation. They extend their love to all.

11 — 22 This means that two masters are present, one of whom will cling more to the material than the spiritual. For these people to be effective, they should have another strong active number that provides a definite focal point from which they can operate.

33 — 11 Two master numbers are present here. These people possess great vision and could become the head in any field in which they have interests. Perhaps music is an interest. If law is your field you could possibly win your argument on your closing speech.

33 — 22 Again, two master numbers are present. These numbers might prove to be a heavy burden of responsibility. Whatever your field, you will endeavour to be the very best you can be.

Chapter 3

CHARTING
A LIFE

*To interpret the life of a person, we create a chart,
and place thereon the numbers or digits comprising the
birthdate. We then read the meaning of these numbers,
and the general appearance of the chart so written.*

NUMBERS AND THEIR INFLUENCES, HETTIE TEMPLETON

It is very easy to create a numerology birthdate (or life) chart. The skill comes in reading and interpreting this chart in conjunction with all other aspects of the person's number vibrations: ruling number, day number, personal year number, pyramid chart and name numbers.

To make the chart, simply draw two parallel horizontal lines across two parallel vertical lines. This creates nine squares and also makes three planes known as mind, soul and body, representing the grand triunion of life.

THOUGHT   WILL   ACTION

CONSCIOUS MIND

SOUL: EMOTIONS, FAITH

EARTH: MATERIAL REALM, PHYSICAL BODY

To claim that the above chart represents a life may sound absurd but it is a reminder that numbers do not give life. Mind, soul and body are born to all. The numbers on each plane provide a reliable indication of the individual's prevailing vibrations. Each individual is capable of thought, will and action. How these attributes balance and interact for an individual is evident from the chart.

The digits of the birthdate are written on the chart in the following positions, and each number has its own particular meaning — as we already know.

3	6	9
2	5	8
1	4	7

This chart, with a number in each square, is perfect. But no person is perfect, and the missing numbers in a birthdate reveal apparent imperfections or, more accurately, areas the person needs to focus on or address during their lifetime. Where numbers are missing, the gap represents the characteristics that are weak and need to be strengthened. If there is a zero in the birthdate, it does not appear on the chart, although zeros in a birthdate intensify all other numbers. Multiple occurrences of any number also affect the interpretation and meaning of the chart.

Persons who have all the numbers on any one of the three planes (mind, soul or body) have a balanced expression on that plane. Some charts with fewer numbers might appear weak, but people with the weakest of charts, if correctly trained and guided, can live constructively and often make a better success of life than people with stronger charts.

It is interesting to note that babies born in the first decade of the 21st century can have up to eight squares empty, including all three on the bottom row or earth plane. Many of them are likely to be exceptionally sensitive and spiritual, attributes that can be of great value to humanity in these times of religion-based conflict and climatic challenges.

The birthdate 4/6/1952 will appear like this:

	6	9
2	5	
1	4	

Note that each plane is fairly evenly balanced, mentally, emotionally and physically.

Often, one or more squares on a chart will contain more than a single number, as seen with the birthdate 2/4/1943, for example. The two number 4s are placed in the same square.

3		9
2		
1	44	

Note that in this chart there are four empty squares.

In the birthdate 10/11/1951 there are five 1s, and the chart for this is set out as follows:

		9
	5	
11111		

Note that there are six empty spaces.

THE MEANINGS OF THE NUMBERS ON THE CHART

Remember that to gain a full understanding of a person's strengths and weaknesses, the numbers on the chart must be read in conjunction with all other aspects.

1 ON THE CHART

The number 1 on the chart always relates to the self. It is the initial number on the material / earth plane.

1 plays a great part in many birthdates in the 20th century. For these people, there can be as many as seven in one birthdate, and there is always at least one 1. By contrast, many of those born in the 21st century will have no 1 on their chart.

ONE 1
This indicates a weakness of verbal self-explanation. This does
not mean that these people cannot speak well — they often
become orators, but they rarely win arguments affecting
themselves unless they know the subject of the argument very
well. They don't seem able to give lucid explanations of their
own conduct or attitudes when suddenly confronted.

TWO 1S
People with two 1s carry the gift of balanced verbal self-
expression. They have the ability to instantly see both sides
of any situation, enabling them to advocate the point of
view they want to support.

THREE 1S
Many of these people are known as 'chatterboxes' and are
often good public speakers while others, who are quiet in
speech, find their best expression through some form of
music or writing. Often, people with three 1s have no
numbers on the soul plane (2, 5, 8).

FOUR 1S
These people are often greatly misunderstood because of
their inability to express themselves. This leads to many hurts
and heartaches but they hide their feelings behind a smile.
They think deeply about other people but their super-sensitivity
can lead to a confused expression of those thoughts, causing
their kindly intentions to be misunderstood.

FIVE OR MORE 1S

This is a more exaggerated form of having four 1s. These people find it very difficult to express themselves clearly except through writing or some form of art. Their early lives are usually sad because they are not lucid when verbally expressing their thoughts and feelings, which means they bottle up lots of unused energy. They can feel inadequate and because of this, may turn to some type of stimulant, such as alcohol, to instil bravado. They are acutely sensitive and think people are always 'looking at them'.

2 ON THE CHART

People with this number in their chart are sensitive and intuitive. Sitting at the forefront of the soul plane, these number 2 qualities can develop into awareness and good people skills as the individual matures. It is worth noting that all children born in the 21st century will have at least one 2 in their chart, which is likely to contribute to an increased global sensitivity and awareness as these children age and begin to form the majority of the world population.

ONE 2

Some of these people are so sensitive they can be easily hurt and their lives may need some guidance, which can often be found through their ruling numbers.

TWO 2S

Sensitivity and intuition are accentuated and these people seem able to form very reliable first impressions. If they follow their intuition or first impressions they will have clearer visions of their plans. They can easily detect sincerity or insincerity in others. These people like to be involved in good causes where they see a need to help others but, in doing this, must take care not to neglect their loved ones. Children with two 2s are quick to imitate and follow any example set before them.

THREE 2S

These people are often absorbed in a world of their own and can become known as dreamers. They can also become too involved with the problems of others.

Some of these people find their way into the entertainment fields, such as acting or playing music. While they may find some success in these forms of expression, they find it difficult to express deep feelings to their close friends and family, and they can be defensive and touchy. This can cause them to feel uncomfortable and to say things that hurt

As children they are hypersensitive and quick to imitate. Parents might help these children achieve self-confidence by following the pathway indicated by the ruling number.

FOUR 2S

These people can often misinterpret their own intuitive feelings, and at times others might not find their reasoning credible. They can be sarcastic, spiteful and bad tempered; alternatively, they might express positive emotions very openly and enthusiastically. Their loved ones need to be understanding and patient. They may overreact in certain situations.

FIVE 2S

These people are often in a state of confusion. They find it difficult to make correct decisions in many areas of their lives and this can lead to a breakdown in relationships, which can ultimately bring on despair. Their best course is often to act on first impressions.

Children with five or more 2s can drive their parents to distraction, and will need constant care and devotion.

3 ON THE CHART

The initial number on the mind plane, 3 strengthens mental activity and stimulates the memory and imagination.

ONE 3

It provides great strength of character and generally indicates a happy nature.

TWO 3S

Two 3s strengthen the imagination. This gives these people the ability to write stories, paint original works of art and do anything requiring strong imagination. But they must learn to discipline this imagination to prevent it running out of control. Although they may find it difficult, meditation is an excellent way for these people to establish control.

Two or more 3s create a restlessness, which is often responsible for headaches.

THREE 3S

These people have difficulty keeping their feet on the ground. They become absorbed in their own thoughts and on planning ahead, leading to confusion when they interact with others. They therefore need guidance to help balance their lives and they should spend as much time as possible in practical activities. They also have a tendency to become argumentative.

FOUR 3S

The imbalance of having four 3s on the chart is a rare occurrence. The last times would have been 1933, on the 3rd, 13th, 23rd, 30th or 31st of March.

These people live in general fear and confusion. They have an impractical outlook on life and may, at some time, need professional help. They often believe their imaginings, which can be wild and vivid, to be true.

People with four 3s need to be encouraged to undertake practical activities. This encourages them to focus. Writing can help put their imagination to work, giving them the potential to enjoy a more balanced life.

4 ON THE CHART

4 is the central number on the earth plane, the plane relating to material and physical wellbeing and activities, including the laying of solid foundations. It indicates a capacity for hard work and practicality.

ONE 4

People with one 4 are usually active, practical, tidy and well organised. They can sometimes be sceptical in their outlook, and need to be aware of their choice of words as they can unintentionally seem abrupt. They can become materialistic if there is too much emphasis on the physical side of life.

TWO 4S

These people have a tendency to relate everything to the physical. It is a peculiarity of these people that they often have trouble with their feet and ankles. They often meet obstacles and challenges in their material lives, which can have the effect of delaying any intended spiritual development. Learning to have a more balanced outlook would make their lives happier. These people would benefit from having a ruling number or name number from the soul plane (2, 5, 8) or from the mental plane (3, 6, 9).

THREE OR FOUR 4S

Having this many 4s compounds all that has been said of two 4s. These people find life rather difficult and there may be a tendency to work with seemingly no respite. They should try to avoid becoming obsessed with their work or with keeping things neat and tidy. They also need to take care when doing sport or exercise, as they may have a weakness in their lower limbs.

Some people with three or four 4s might like to balance their hard work with pastimes of a completely opposite nature. They might, for example, read books that help to uplift the heart and soul, or take time out to sit in quiet contemplation or listen to soothing music.

5 ON THE CHART

5 is the central number on the soul plane and in the column of the will. It comes into direct contact with every other number, giving balance to the personality and helping with emotional control. The number 5 provides strength of character and is a powerful number whether it occurs on the chart or as a ruling number.

ONE 5

One 5 on the chart aids a good understanding of the self and others. These people have the power of endurance, courage and compassion. To push them too hard as children would be to turn them into young tyrants.

TWO 5S

These people have lots of enthusiasm, which can often become intense and overbearing. They also have an air of assurance and great confidence about them that usually fades as they mature. Their enthusiasm causes mis-understandings and has a tendency to cause domestic troubles. If this driving intensity can be controlled they will have clearer vision and avoid many mistakes.

Because these people are so intense, they suffer emotional turmoil, often bringing on stomach ulcers and indigestion and possibly other associated health problems. These people can also be accident prone.

THREE OR FOUR 5S

What is said of two 5s also applies here. But people with three or four 5s suffer an emotional intensity that is very difficult to live with. They are impulsive and need to think before they speak or act to help avoid remarks that may be offensive.

Those people born on 5th, 15th or 25th of May 1955 will have four 5s on their chart.

6 ON THE CHART

This is known as the number of creativity, and also stands for love of the home.

ONE 6

These people are artistic in many fields and have a special love of the home. If they don't have their own home they will interest themselves in the home of someone else. They like home responsibilities and have the ability to create the atmosphere of home.

TWO 6S
These make people very unsettled and over-anxious about their homes. They worry about them and their families, and this affects their nervous system. Because they use so much nervous energy, they need lots of rest and need to practise relaxation to calm their nerves.

THREE OR FOUR 6S
Having so many 6s on the chart will magnify the home worries and if care is not taken these people could make themselves ill with nervous problems. They tend to allow the home to possess them and to be over protective and loving of the people in the home, which can have a smothering effect.

Four 6s compounds the above effects on people who, by their perpetual worrying, can destroy their own health.

7 ON THE CHART
This is regarded as a mystical number with infinite possibilities. It is related to learning life's lessons via sacrifice and suffering, usually in a very human way because of 7's position as the final number on the earth plane.

ONE 7

These people will experience some type of upheaval in the home, which will lead to some form of sacrifice. Whatever the sacrifices, they are intended for the development of the soul and to be accepted as lessons.

TWO OR THREE 7S

When these people are living optimistically and positively they show a wonderful understanding of others' problems and have the power to give them help and comfort.

If they are pessimistic or negative, these people will constantly complain about their losses, blame others, and think of themselves as victims. Again, where there are 7s on the birthdate chart, it means sacrifice — possibly in love, money or health. Until they learn their life lesson — that their problems are self-inflicted because of the choices they make — they will face the same challenges repeatedly. This pattern is likely to continue until they become aware and make the necessary changes in attitude and action.

FOUR 7S

This many 7s intensify the compounded sacrifices these people must face, and their family members will probably also feel the impact. The most recent generation of people with four 7s were born on the 7th, 17th or 27th of July 1977; there will not be another batch until the 7th, 17th or 27th of July 2077. People with four 7s need deep understanding and should be guided to look on the positive side of life. For those whose attitude is positive and who are awake and aware, these numbers give wonderful potential for philosophical understanding and the raising of spiritual consciousness.

8 ON THE CHART

Located on the soul plane in the column of action, 8 is the number of insight, wisdom and initiative carried through into practical actions.

ONE 8

This makes these people very restless, yet they have good reasoning power. It makes them meticulous and attentive to detail, methodical and tidy.

TWO 8S

These people have the same qualities of one 8 and generally move about a good deal in their early lives. They usually have a great desire to travel, feeling the need to gain understanding of life through personal experiences. If they do not have the opportunity to travel when young, they may feel frustrated and irritable until they are able to travel, and this will bring them some peace of mind.

THREE 8S

These multiple numbers can mean a lot of trouble in these people's lives, especially when they reach their 40s. As they enter their 50s they leave all these troubles behind but they can never regain lost opportunities. They need encouragement to enjoy a positive outlook on life.

9 ON THE CHART

A mind number in the column of action, 9 relates to idealism and the capacity to act on it.

ONE 9

These people are idealists with the tenacity to succeed at whatever goal they choose, whether this is of a material or an idealistic nature. They tend to throw the whole of their interest and energy into whatever they take up, sometimes to the exclusion of everything else. They should take care not to allow their pursuit of perfection to dominate their lives.

TWO 9S

These two numbers together indicate people who are deep thinkers. They must watch that they do not become unduly critical, yet there is always a kindly thought behind whatever they do or say.

THREE 9S

These make the mental plane over-represented. Such people should be trained to look at situations calmly, and to see above the petty things of life. They must endeavour to refrain from outbursts of temper because they will be liable to lose control.

With children, never promise or suggest anything too far ahead of time because anticipation and waiting makes them extremely anxious. If concentration at school becomes a problem because they feel over-loaded, a calendar or diary, where they list and mark off activities and goals, can help these children to manage their lives with less stress.

FOUR 9S

There are two definite personality types here. The first tries to conform to society then will suddenly rebel and hide away, perhaps staying indoors for days or weeks. They are usually the quiet types, who do not respond well to any form of advice or guidance.

The second of these types enjoys belittling others who don't share their beliefs. They can fly into a rage and need careful counselling to prevent them harming themselves or someone else.

ISOLATED NUMBERS ON THE CHART

Numbers can occur in isolation on the chart when there is no 5. When this happens, the isolated number has a specific impact. Some people born in the 20th century will have an isolated 1, 3, 7 or 9, while some born in the 21st century will have an isolated 2, 7, 8 or 9.

If there are multiple isolated numbers in the one square, the challenges will probably be compounded.

Example birthday: 3 August 1967 (the 1 is isolated)

3	6	9
		8
1		7

Example birthday: 8 March 2001 (the 8 is isolated)

3		
2		8
1		

ISOLATED 1

There is no 2, 4 or 5 on the birthdate chart. This person is likely to feel detached or cut off from others. Because the number 1 represents the self, no matter how well or how much they explain themselves, they will feel misunderstood.

ISOLATED 2

There is no 1, 3, 4, 5 or 6 on the birthdate chart. These people will flounder until they find a point of reference, possibly in their ruling, day or name numbers, from which they can balance themselves. They are likely to be timid and must learn to assert themselves in a group if they wish to find happiness.

ISOLATED 3

There is no 2, 5 or 6 on the birthdate chart. This means that the thoughts and ideas of this person can disconnect and dissolve quickly. If these people have a great idea, they need to write it down immediately, or there is a good chance that it will be forgotten or confused by the time they get to it.

ISOLATED 7

There is no 4, 5 or 8 on the birthdate chart. Repeated lessons of the same kind occur for these people until commonsense prevails and they realise what they are doing wrong. Until this happens, life is painful for them.

ISOLATED 8

There is no 4, 5, 6, 7 or 9 on the birthdate chart. These people will feel extremely isolated and misunderstood. They deeply desire independence but will find it difficult to achieve until they assert willpower, ambition and ideals.

ISOLATED 9

There is no 5, 6 or 8 on the birthdate chart. This can produce unfulfilled ambition (one 9) or foolish idealism (two 9s). If there are more than two 9s then both might prevail.

Chapter 4

THE
ARROWS

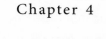

Adversity brings knowledge, and knowledge wisdom.

WELSH PROVERB

Ultimately, what we do with our lives is greatly affected by our attitude and the way in which it influences the decisions and choices we make. An understanding of our numbers simply provides clarity and insight to assist us in making those decisions. Those who are drawn to studying numerology in some depth can look beyond the simple interpretation of the numbers on the chart to patterns revealed within it.

After constructing the chart of a birthdate and studying the weighting of numbers on it, a numerologist then examines it for specific features known as arrows, where every square in a row, column or diagonal is completely full or completely empty. There are 15 possible arrows, and the 16th option of a chart with no arrows.

The arrows, full and empty, indicate specific characteristics that can be considered in combination with the person's ruling number. A 'full' arrow always adds impact and assists the ruling number, while an 'empty' arrow indicates weakness in a particular area, highlighting the need for that individual to pay special attention to it.

Some charts have more than one arrow, either full or empty, or even one or more of both. If we look at a chart with one, two or more empty arrows, we will initially be aware of potential weaknesses. This need not be cause for alarm. In such situations, awareness of the challenges can spur the person on to greater achievements and a successful life. On the other hand, a person who has one, two or more full arrows in their chart risks becoming complacent, allowing opportunities to pass them by.

Further on in this chapter, each arrow is described in detail. But while each arrow provides information and guidance in its own right, like all other aspects of numerology, it reveals even more when considered in a broader context. For example, the chart for a birthdate of 9 August 2005 has one full arrow and very few other numbers. The arrow is of great benefit.

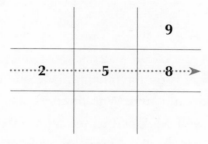

On the other hand, the chart for a birthdate of 19 September 2006 has one empty arrow.

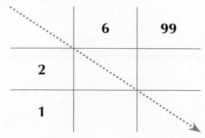

A thorough understanding of the other numbers on the chart indicates which strengths and attributes the person has to work with. Then, when they examine and understand the challenges presented by their empty arrow, they know what inner resources they can call on.

There will be occasions when the chart has a full arrow together with an empty arrow, for example for the birthdate 1 January 1963:

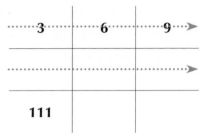

The strength here is on the mental plane and the weakness is on the emotional plane. With three 1s also on the chart, this person is well equipped to see all sides of an issue or situation and express their thoughts clearly. Unless taken suddenly off guard, they can apply this ability along with their steady, reliable mental state to counteract any emotional overreactions that might occur as a result of hypersensitivity.

Another example stems from the birthdate 19 July 2003:

This person's strength lies in the thoughtful planning arrow (full 1, 2, 3) while their challenges lie in a lack of willpower (empty 4, 5, 6). Applying the idealism of their isolated 9 and their capacity to learn from mistakes (isolated 7), they can create a 'bridge' to carry their plans across the empty willpower 'gap' and activate them. While this might be difficult, awareness of challenges and strengths will make it easier for the person to achieve success.

A final example shows a chart with two empty arrows and one full arrow (birthdate 5 August 2002):

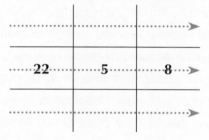

This child will feel everything through the soul plane and may live in a world dominated by emotion. Throughout life, this person will rely purely on intuition in most situations. Lacking 1, 4, 7 on the earth plane and 3, 6, 9 on the mental plane, they will be inclined to live in an ungrounded fantasy realm. They might find themselves feeling nervy and unwell from time to time. Involvement with the world of nature and regular physical and mental exercise will help them to remain balanced.

THE ARROW OF DETERMINATION
Birthdate of Kirstie Alley, actress: 12/1/1955

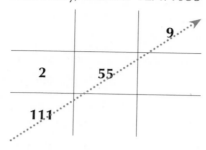

In this chart the arrow through the numbers 1, 5, 9 indicates a spirit of determination. Such people are noted for their persistence and endurance, and will go to almost any extent to achieve their objectives. In many circumstances this can be a fine characteristic but people with this arrow must cultivate patience and guard against outbreaks of temper which can flare should they meet obstacles. If they fail too often to control their actions they may become inflexible and even cruel.

Children with this chart are very high-spirited and strong-willed, and do not always respond well to discipline. Their tendency to argue should be seen not as stubbornness, but as attempts to express themselves clearly. Parents are best advised not to drive such children but to persuade them with reason. They will respond better to this type of approach, especially when executed with affection and patience. Bullying could break their spirits and destroy any desire they might have to achieve worthwhile goals.

THE ARROW OF HESITATION

Birthdate example: 6/7/2003

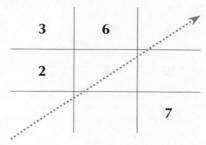

This arrow indicates the absence of the numbers 1, 5, 9 and is the opposite of the arrow of determination. It last occurred during the 9th century, and is now occurring for some children born in the 21st century. The separation in the chart creates a powerful force leading to procrastination. These people will find themselves leaving work half completed or not even beginning tasks that may be considered essential. This can aggravate personal relationships and can greatly annoy even the person possessing this trait.

Children with this arrow must be trained to develop perseverance and patience. Efforts in this should begin while the children are very young, even by deliberately giving them small tasks to complete. They must be encouraged not to lose heart and shown that the final results are worth the effort.

The arrow of mysticism
Birthdate example: 23/7/1952

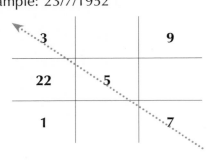

The numbers 3, 5, 7, aligned along this arrow, indicate the presence of mysticism. People with this arrow possess an understanding and interest in spiritual questions connected to subjects such as religion and mysticism. To friends they may appear to live sad lives, and indeed they do experience a lot of sorrow. But their experience with adversity, if confronted with patience and intelligence, will give them serenity and understanding that is beyond price. Generally, these people prefer to think their own way through difficulties and do not take kindly to advice.

Children with this arrow often suffer in silence and yet they are observant and insightful about what is happening around them. This makes it even more important than usual for parents to be forthcoming and honest in their dealings with these children who are quick to notice deception or dishonesty. They also need guidance and affection to give them courage and confidence they may otherwise lack.

THE ARROW OF SCEPTICISM AND ORTHODOXY

Birthdate of Stephen Hawking, physicist: 8/1/1942

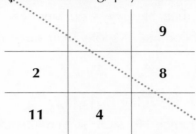

This arrow indicates that there are no numbers 3, 5, 7. Although these have been called the numbers of mysticism, their absence does not mean that these people will not be spiritually inclined. They are very loving and just, but they often find it hard to express themselves in any way. Writing or art are often their best avenues of expression.

These people are known as sceptics and because of this, they have a curiosity that may often lead them to explore specific issues.

This arrow is often responsible for all kinds of head troubles, such as headaches, bad eyes, or head accidents — if not to the person, then to someone associated with them. They may have to care for someone with these problems or have such a person dependent upon them. They seem to worry, which again might bring on these head troubles. They have a very kindly, gentle nature.

Children with this chart are often moody and sometimes want to be left alone. Within reason, parents should observe their wishes in this direction. They are very loving and are dependent for their happiness on kindness from others. If this is not forthcoming, it spoils their outlook on life.

THE ARROW OF THE INTELLECT
Birthdate of Whitney Houston, singer/entertainer: 9/8/1963

```
······3·············6·············99···➤
      |           |
──────┼───────────┼──────────
      |           |        8
──────┼───────────┼──────────
   1  |           |
```

This arrow indicates that the mind plane, 3, 6, 9, is completely filled, giving a well-balanced mind and a very good memory. The dominant quality of these people is balance, although their strength in this direction may make them intolerant when they contact others who lack this quality. If they wish to avoid offence, they will have to make the effort to understand weaknesses and failings in others. Despite this tendency to be critical, these people are happiest when in company and especially enjoy doing things to help others. Adequate rest is important for these people, who rely a lot on their thinking power. They will find that revitalisation will come easier with quiet meditation or by listening to soothing music. They often find that life brings added home responsibilities, which they are able to carry well.

These children usually have good memories and strong intellect and should be given every chance to choose a tertiary education. Some of their energies should be directed towards music or art and outdoor activity to ensure they don't become obsessed with purely mental activity.

Parents will sometimes find these children headstrong and difficult to understand. Consequent problems are best counteracted by calming the children with small duties and by showing appreciation for their efforts. They won't forget such appreciative attention.

Without adequate parental direction these children tend to become selfish, which is simply an expression of their need for attention. If they exhibit the appearance of loneliness the best that parents can do is to express their love and explain that everyone, not only themselves, feels occasional neglect and hurt. They should be helped to value their intuition instead of relying entirely on facts and logic — especially in relationships with their peers.

THE ARROW OF POOR MEMORY
Birthdate of Artur Rubenstein, musician: 28/1/1887

2		888
11		7

This arrow indicates an empty head / mind plane. The absence of 3, 6 and 9 in this chart does not mean that these people are not intelligent — but it does have other consequences. They are often very clever and witty and many become executives in big business organisations, but whatever their course in life, they must keep their minds active, not only in material matters, but also interests of an artistic or deeper nature. A lack of such mental activity can result in these people, by the time they reach middle age, losing interest in life and in later life suffering loss of memory.

Children with this chart may appear backward at first. There is nothing to be alarmed about, for they soon make up for lost time. They may complain of headaches, but they usually outgrow this problem by the time they are seven years of age. This may affect early schooling and parents should be patient when scrutinising their children's study efforts. In general these children are sweet, loving and sincere.

THE ARROW OF EMOTIONAL BALANCE

Birthdate example: 28/2/1958

```
                        |              |
                        |              |   9
        _____|_____|_____
        ....22.........|......5.......|....88...▶
        _____|_____|_____
             1          |              |
                        |              |
```

This arrow indicates that the soul plane 2, 5, 8 is filled. These people are observant and possess a sensitivity that promotes reasonableness in their relationships with others. They can readily enter into the spirit of things, immediately seeing the other person's point of view. But, paradoxically, their sensitivity can lead to feelings of isolation which often result in depression. Fortunately, they have the power to recover quickly and episodes of loneliness or depression can be minimised if they make a conscious effort to be more gregarious and interest themselves in a special pastime or hobby. Because they are susceptible to the influence of their environment they should make a point of mixing with other people to bring as much brightness and laughter as possible into their lives.

Their soul intensity carries with it a healing power so that, with concentration and care, they can use this healing power in any positive way they choose. If they allow their strong intuition to guide them, they will feel less sensitive and be more sure of themselves.

Children with this arrow will suffer with nervous stomach disorders. Being very impressionable, they are greatly affected by their environment and their lives will be shaped, more than usually, by their home conditions. They have empathy for those who are suffering but will also suffer if they feel they are not understood or loved. Should this occur, they will stand defiantly against everyone. The best remedy in this situation is for parents to show their trust, encourage the child to talk things over and ensure that a loving atmosphere prevails in the home. With such abundant sensitivity, the child will easily use up their reserves of soul energy. As love is the food on which the soul thrives, these children will also thrive on lots of love, hugs, cuddles and understanding.

Many of these children lag behind in schoolwork, giving the impression of being dreamers, although this is often a consequence of their attempts to avoid disharmony. They may also experience a setback in health, so it is necessary to keep as much brightness as possible in their lives. They are susceptible to expressions of both joy and sadness and experience these feelings with intensity.

They should be discouraged from any strange habits such as tapping their fingers or twirling their hair. Such behaviour can annoy others and if not discouraged, can easily remain with them into adulthood.

THE ARROW OF HYPERSENSITIVITY

Birthdate of Gough Whitlam, former Australian prime minister: 11/7/1916

6		9
1111		7

This arrow indicates the soul plane is empty of the numbers 2, 5, 8. This does not mean that the person has no soul but that the soul has no natural protection. This causes these people to close up within themselves, in self-defence, and this is often mistaken by others as stubbornness. They are loving, sensitive, tender and very easily hurt. Because of their propensity to suffer an inferiority complex, they often misrepresent themselves and misunderstand others. Rather than stew over decisions, they would avoid many misunderstandings if they based their judgments and actions on first (intuitional) impressions, and talked out any problems or issues.

Children with this arrow are sensitive and shy. They are always yearning for someone to love them and parents should never put off listening to their questions or complaints. They should never be criticised in the presence of others — rather, they should be encouraged in every way to have trust in all that their parents say. This approach will give them the strength to face the obstacles they will inevitably meet in later life.

THE ARROW OF PRACTICALITY AND PHYSICALITY
Birthdate example: 2/4/1970

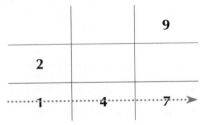

This arrow has the earth plane (1, 4, 7) filled, and these people usually prefer physical activity as opposed to mental activity. They are clever with their hands and make good artisans or talented artists, painters or musicians. They often have a hard life but are nonetheless usually willing to help others in need. Having a ruling number of the soul or mind plane helps allay the tendency of those in non-artistic occupations to become preoccupied with material gain.

People with this arrow are often poor judges of character and when personal relations go wrong, they can become angry or even violent, depending on the amount of frustration in their lives and on their ruling number. They may also be verbally hurtful, but can control these traits if they put their mind to it.

These people are able to hide their sensitivity but this does not mean that they have not felt the impact of the pain or joy in a given situation.

Children with this arrow need to be encouraged to show love and kindness to those around them. Parents should be alert to the friendships these children form because they can easily be led into trouble which can exacerbate their tendency to solve problems with physical action. It is important to use reason when dealing with these children because issuing demands or using force will only make them rebellious at home and disruptive in the classroom. These children are clever with their hands and should be kept occupied with plenty of toys and materials that offer them the opportunity to use their talents in construction. Make sure they put everything away when they have finished playing. They should also be encouraged to read, especially books about spirituality or animals to help ensure they develop a balanced, healthy outlook.

Any punishment given must be just, and when advice is offered it should never be given in a patronising or vindictive way. Like most children, when they feel understood, they can be very sweet.

THE ARROW OF CONFUSION
Birthdate example: 3/6/2002

3	6	
22		
		→

This arrow, empty of the numbers 1, 4, 7, indicates that such people are not naturally grounded, tending to be over-theoretical in their approach to life. They are frequently criticised for their inability to get things done, or to do well in life. They must strive to appreciate the need to apply themselves diligently to practical tasks and to make sure they complete what they start. Failure to do so can lead to much confusion and disorder in their lives, possibly resulting in their dependence on social security or charity.

Children with this arrow must be trained from infancy to always complete tasks — perhaps the old proverb 'if a job is worth doing it is worth doing well' applies here. A good practice is to take a genuine interest in their schoolwork and to always check that their homework is finished. The same applies to domestic chores. No matter how tedious it may become, parents should not simply assume that these children have completed their tasks. This approach requires much patience, but the goal — to train children to remain focused on practical tasks — is worthy of the effort.

When a task is done well, give a reward of a practical nature. It is important that these children see and feel their reward.

THE ARROW OF ACTIVITY
Example birthdate: 21/6/1987

This arrow comprises the three highest numbers, 7, 8, 9, and fills the action column of the chart, offering a combination of learning through sacrifice (7), leading to perceptiveness (8) and ambition (9).

People with this arrow are inclined to be hyperactive. They like to be always busy. They prefer a peaceful existence and dread confrontation, too much of which can actually make them ill. It is not uncommon for them to suffer from headaches, digestive upsets, or heart / circulatory problems. Awareness of these predispositions offers them the opportunity to choose a healthy diet, exercise and lifestyle options. Learning to play a musical instrument, or writing, can help them immeasurably.

Children with this arrow are mentally active. If they worry when they are very young or are raised in disturbing conditions they can experience many setbacks. If they are upset about something, talk it over immediately and allay their fears and concerns.

These children need peaceful surroundings, without which they are likely to fall sick. Always take note when they say they don't want to go to school: apart from any physical illness, they might have experienced some slight altercation with a teacher or fellow-student. Take time to investigate and resolve whatever has caused the disturbance.

These children need plenty of outdoor life, even to the extent of eating outdoors whenever possible. They thrive in a calm environment and also need more rest than the average child.

THE ARROW OF INACTIVITY
Birthdate example: 2/5/2006

	6	↑
22	5	

The absence of the numbers 7, 8, 9 (in the column of action) in this chart indicates a weakness in the ability to persevere with demanding or lengthy tasks. This arrow has not occurred for several centuries, but is once again occurring in the 21st century. For this reason, we will focus initially on how it affects children.

When parents ask these children to do something, they must supervise them to ensure that the job is carried out to the end. This is a huge job for parents, especially if these children also have no numbers on the will plane (absence of the numbers 4, 5, 6). Training must begin as soon as these children can understand a pointed finger or a frown.

Involvement in sport will help teach them the benefits of teamwork and give them a sense of achievement — characteristics they will need as adults.

As they mature, these people should be made aware of this particular challenge; otherwise they will fail to realise their full potential. They have a great ability to think and plan but learn best by experience, so active engagement in their chosen field provides them with the most effective learning environment. They must consciously work at developing perseverance and avoiding passivity, especially as this will be interpreted by others as laziness. Even as adults, they will continue to find participation in sport a great boon to their development.

THE ARROW OF THE WILL
Birthdate of Cate Blanchett, actress: 14/5/1969

	6	99
	5	
11	4	

This arrow indicates that the centre squares, 4, 5 and 6, are filled, giving these people an exceptionally strong will which enables them to overcome many problems. Once they make up their minds to do something they just go ahead and do it, even though it could mean riding roughshod over the wishes of others. At times their desires are only fleeting, thus creating an inclination in them to forget tomorrow what they believed important today. They would find it helpful to take up interests that include interacting with others because this might encourage them to express themselves.

Although the characteristics mentioned above could lead to self-centredness and criticism from their peers, they do not lessen the ability of these people to cultivate and maintain true friendships.

Children with this arrow on their chart often hurt the feelings of others with their strong opinions and desire to always have their own way. From a very early age, they should be encouraged to respect other people's views and to understand that they themselves are not always right. Another way of helping these children would be to show them — perhaps by example — that small deeds of kindness, besides having their own intrinsic value, can help win friendship and respect from others.

It is important to keep in mind that despite their outward wilfulness, these children are well-meaning, and any treatment they perceive to be unjust will make them defiant. The most successful parents will be those who avoid reacting harshly to these children's faults and instead cultivate relationships based on love, understanding and logical explanation.

THE ARROW OF FRUSTRATION

Birthdate of Neville Bonner, Australia's first Aboriginal federal politician: 28/3/1922

3		9
222		8
1		

This arrow divides the chart vertically. The absence of numbers 4, 5, 6 indicates one or another form of loss. Sometimes it means there is loneliness, which might have no obvious cause, although knowledge of numerology can help to bring an understanding of such conditions. In other cases it indicates separation or broken home conditions. These people often experience loneliness and sadness caused by disappointment in friendships.

Because the column of the will is empty, they need to acquire the skill of building a mental bridge to carry their plans and ideas (1, 2, 3) across into action (7, 8, 9). Those who are aware of the challenge in this arrow, and who choose to work at this skill, do much better in life than those who remain unaware.

Children with the arrow of frustration on their chart sometimes become overly dependent on their parents or teachers, largely because their inability to carry ideas to fruition erodes their self-confidence. They should be treated with patience and tenderness, supported in activities that help them develop a sense of self-worth and self-reliance, and motivated to complete their chores. When these children set their hearts on a particular goal, parents can use this powerful motivation as a tool for helping them to activate their ideas and dreams. The resultant feeling of achievement will help strengthen their ability to cope with life and thrive.

THE ARROW OF THE PLANNER
Birthdate of Harrison Ford, actor: 13/7/1942

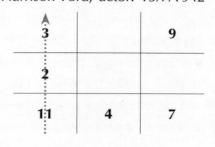

This arrow indicates the inclusion of the numbers 1, 2, 3. This denotes love of order in their personal possessions and concerns. Yet curiously enough, they are untidy in general ways. In other words, they like order in their surroundings but do not want the trouble of creating it. This tendency to ignore the mundane is also expressed in the handling of their occupational tasks. Yet when it comes to big tasks, they assert themselves and demonstrate organisational skills of a high level. These people would strengthen their relationships at work and at home by learning the value of getting the small details right.

Children with this chart should be taught right from the beginning to be tidy and to respect the ideas, possessions and habits of others. They often take too much for granted and are slow to appreciate the offence this can give to others. Despite their restlessness and self-absorption they are trusting of authority figures. They are very restless, giving them an unsettled feeling and this can make them nervous.

Illustrated books can be very helpful in subduing their unrest.

Note *that there is no arrow that shows the empty squares on the plane of the planner: 1, 2, 3. Since the 11th century to the end of the 20th century, there has always been at least one 1 on that plane. For the next couple of millennia, this plane will not be empty because there will be at the very least a 2 or 3 on that plane. Therefore, for now, there is no arrow for the empty plane of the planner.*

No ARROWS
Birthdate of Wolfgang Mozart: 27/1/1756

	6	
2	5	
11		77

The lack of arrows on a chart indicates a lack of specific strengths or challenges, which can present a challenge in itself. While these people can adapt well to most social and workplace situations, they often find it difficult to muster sufficient enthusiasm to involve themselves deeply in any particular project. They may slide through life without making waves and without any outstanding achievements either. Often, they lack the energy or motivation to be assertive. Such people would do well to look towards their ruling number, day number or name number for direction and strength.

Children who have a chart with no arrows are usually well adjusted and easy-going but their wellbeing should not be taken for granted. They should be encouraged to be more definite in expressing their opinions, especially with matters they care about. Parents who support development of particular interests, hobbies or skills in such children will find they can use this as a basis for helping them communicate assertively.

Chapter 5

NAMES AND
NAMING

*The name by which a person is constantly called
and known plays a great part, and is an immense
influence, in shaping his or her character and life.*

NUMBERS AND THEIR INFLUENCE, HETTIE TEMPLETON

Everything in our world is vibrating, and letters of the alphabet (in any language) are no exception. Each letter, vibrating in perfect harmony with all others, has a particular frequency that resonates with a particular number. By charting and analysing the numbers of a name — or a collection of names — in a range of different ways, we can deepen our understanding of ourselves or another individual.

While the numbers of our birthdate are fixed and cannot be altered, we do have the power to choose the vibrational influence of names. Parents who are aware of this can use numerological understanding to ensure that the name they give their child harmonises with and complements the vibrations of the child's birthdate chart, ruling number and day number.

Similarly, if an adult feels unhappy with their name, or feels that its vibration is not comfortable or positive for them, when they understand the numerological value of each of the letters, they can choose a name that they feel serves them better.

The meanings and weightings of main name numbers are the same as those given for ruling numbers: they have a pervasive influence throughout the person's lifetime. Sound of any kind has a tremendous impact on the nervous system. Every time a name is called or spoken it sets up a wavelength or vibration that either soothes or irritates.

Bear in mind that *the name that counts most is the one by which a person is usually called*, whether it is the first name, a pet name or a nickname. This is the everyday name that will set up live vibrations. (A second / middle name which is rarely if ever used does not vibrate into life; it is, in essence, dead.)

The surname or family name is the next most important name because it is also frequently used.

For those who wish to explore their name vibrations in greater depth, from the consonants in the name, we can work out the person's *outer expression* (personality, and the aspects readily visible to other people); from the vowels, their *soul urge* (which reveals emotional and spiritual aspects). Finally, if we consider the entire name as it appears on the person's birth certificate, we obtain their *destiny number* (indicating their place in the world).

CALCULATING THE NUMBERS OF A NAME

The following table shows the number associated with each letter of our alphabet.

1	2	3	4	5	6	7	8	9
A	B	C	D	E	F	G	H	I
J	K	L	M	N	O	P	Q	R
S	T	U	V	W	X	Y	Z	

We can also arrange this information differently to show which plane — mind, soul or earth / physical — each letter belongs to:

Mind	Soul	Earth / physical
C 3	B 2	A 1
L 3	K 2	J 1
U 3	T 2	S 1
F 6	E 5	D 4
O 6	N 5	M 4
X 6	W 5	V 4
I 9	H 8	G 7
R 9	Q 8	P 7
	Z 8	Y 7

When drawing up a chart for name numbers, it is important to view it in conjunction with the person's birthdate chart. This will show clearly whether the two vibrational fields are harmonious and balanced, or whether the individual might be wise to consider changing their name in some way.

In general, when the birthdate chart is strong, it should be balanced with a weaker name; and when a birthdate chart is weak, strength must be added through the name.

Working this out is not as difficult as it might sound.

Example birthdate: 23/7/1960.

Ruling number: 2 + 3 + 7 + 1 + 9 + 6 = 28 = 10.

Day number: 2 + 3 = 5.

The birthdate chart looks like this:

3	6	9
2		
1		7

This individual's everyday name is Michael (he is not known as or called Mike).

Using the conversion chart, note the numerical value of each of the vowels and consonants, thus:

```
   9        1  5
M  I  C  H  A  E  L
4     3  8        3
```

Michael's name chart looks like this:

33		9
	5	8
1	4	

When we view the birthdate chart and name chart together, we see that they are well balanced.

Birthdate chart		
3	6	9
2		
1		7

Name chart		
33		9
	5	8
1	4	

Combined chart		
333	6	99
2	5	8
11	4	7

We can also see that the combination gives Michael a good imagination: his birthdate chart has one 3 and his name chart has two 3s, making three 3s. Also, there are two 9s and two 1s. Michael's inner urge (soul urge, from the vowels) is 15: 1 + 5 = 6. The outer expression (from the consonants) is 18: 1 + 8 = 9. When the soul urge and outer expression are added to make 15, the name number is revealed to be 6 (1 + 5 = 6). To understand the impact of this name number of 6, read the information on ruling number 6 (see page 41).

SOUL URGE

It is generally thought that the vowels (A, E, I, O, U) are the life or soul of every word. Among Polynesian peoples the reason for the beauty, softness and rhythm of their speech and song is due to the many vowels used in every word, and the fact that almost every word ends with a vowel.

The soul or inner urge numbers are taken from the vowels in your everyday name. This must be the name by which you are constantly called, whether it is your given name, an abbreviation, a nickname or even initials like AJ, for example.

Add the numbers related to the vowels in your everyday name. If you are called Jan there is one vowel, the A, which equals the number 1. If you are called Bob, there is one vowel, the O, which equals the number 6. In the name Michael, there are three vowels, I, A, E, which totals 15, resulting in 1 + 5 = 6. If this man prefers to be called Mike, the two vowels are I and E which total 14, resulting in 1 + 4 = 5.

MEANINGS OF THE SOUL OR INNER URGE NUMBERS

1   You long for individual freedom. Your ruling number can influence the area in which you exercise this freedom.

2   Harmony and balance are important to you. Your intuition is strong.

3   Whether in business or social activities, you are quick to assess / feel a situation.

4   You are orderly in your outlook on many subjects, and not prone to emotional displays.

5   You have a deep need for freedom of thought and a strong urge to express this.

6   In whatever you do, the need to create is strong. Take care that you do not use this energy to create unnecessary worries or anxieties.

7   We human beings are here to help and teach each other. You, 'the teacher', must remember this.

8   You feel the need for independence in thought and action, and must take care not to isolate yourself from family or friends in the pursuit of it.

9   Always show your positive aspects with this number — give out love, be forgiving, be charitable and always be ready to help where you can.

10   This number gives you the opportunity to use your intuition in all its forms, thereby freeing you from mere material / physical thought.

11   Wherever the 11 shows up it indicates spirituality, and here, as a soul urge number, it gives spiritual strength to those attributes you may already have.

22/4   With this master builder number, you are capable of anything — harness this powerful spiritual number to manifest spiritual wisdom here on earth.

33/6   When this number appears it indicates imparting inspiration to others by speech or deed as part of your soul urge.

INFLUENCE OF THE FIRST VOWEL IN A NAME

Where the soul urge number indicates a person's inner feelings and yearnings, the *first vowel* in the name portrays the inner mind, giving an indication of the way the person thinks.

A   It's value is 1, which is the first of the earth numbers, indicating that these people are inclined to think and act alone or independently.

E   It's value is 5 — the central number on the soul plane and the column of the will. These people are

likely to be free-thinkers with very active minds.
They will need to work hard at learning techniques
and skills for staying mentally focused.

I   It's value is 9. This mind number in the action
column gives strength of mind which can become
arrogance. A person with I as their first vowel who
also has a ruling number 9 will need to guard against
self-centredness.

O   It's value is 6. This mind number at the top of the
column of will makes O as an initial vowel a
powerful influence. This strong-minded person can
become very successful if they make the most of the
opportunities that arise in their lives.

U   It's value is 3. This mind number sits in the column
of thought, and those whose initial vowel is U may feel
that they are not as successful as others. They are
usually nice people but they are often misunderstood.

The vowel O (which looks the same as zero) is the most
powerful symbol. This symbol is used as both letter and
number and is found in powerful words such as God, love
and mother. The O begins the compound numbers; it is found
at the beginning of every decade or century. It creates every
hundred and if we go on adding the O, we reach thousands,
millions, billions, and so on to infinity: no beginning, no end.

Here are the vowels in order of their strength:

O	I	A	E	U
6	9	1	5	3

OUTER EXPRESSION

The outer expression number is calculated by adding the numerical value of all the consonants in the person's name. It gives an indication of how the person presents themselves and how they are perceived by others.

Here is an example:

J	O	S	E	P	H	I	N	E
1		1		7	8		5	

When we add the consonant values — 1 + 1 + 7 + 8 + 5 — we get an outer expression number of 22.

If, however, this woman is always called Jo, her outer expression number will be 1 (from the J).

MEANINGS OF THE OUTER EXPRESSION NUMBERS

1   You are positive and usually like to work alone.

2   You are intuitive and like to be part of a group.

3   Ever the entertainer, you are quick-witted and usually happy.

4   You are the practical one and usually not given to sentiment.

5   Freedom to express artistically is your aim. You are fun-loving and usually the life of the party.

6   A lover of home and family, you must learn to express this in a well-balanced way.

7   You love to learn and teach what you know. Remember, you are never alone.

8   You are happy when you are able to express yourself independently. Be daring and confident.

9   Be balanced and positive. Reveal the happy, smiling side of you.

10   You are adaptable and enjoy life. Try not to hurt others with your use of words.

11   Learn to balance your life and harmonise with your surroundings.

22/4   It is important that you find the balance between the spiritual and material in your life. Forget those quick money-making schemes.

33/6   It is important that you continue to remind yourself that nobody is perfect and when you realise that fact, life will be happier for you.

EXAMINING THE LETTER Y

There is sometimes confusion about the letter Y. Some say it is a vowel and others say it is a consonant. Actually, it can be one or the other, depending on its context.

In a name such as Molly, Jody, Candy or Wendy, the Y is counted as a consonant (an outer expression number). Its numerological value is 7.

However, in a name like Lyn, Kydd, Glynn or Hyndmarsh where the first or last name has the Y in the body of the name, the Y is pronounced as a short I or a long I and is a soul urge number with the value of 7.

In the name Sydney, the first Y is considered to be a vowel, while the second, at the end of the word, is counted as a consonant.

CHOOSING OR CHANGING NAMES

Adults change their name for a whole host of reasons: some because they simply don't like it; some because they feel the original name doesn't belong to them; some because they feel a different name will bring them power, fame, good fortune or money; and some choose to change their surname / family name when they marry.

But what about children? They have no say in the matter.

Ideally, the vibrations of a baby's name should harmonise with those of the ruling number and help to balance the birthdate chart. If children are constantly called by names they do not like, they become irritable and upset. Therefore, it is unwise to name them after any particular person unless the name really suits them.

CHOOSING NAMES FOR BABIES

Before choosing a name for your baby, draw up their birthdate chart. (It is interesting to note that many parents, even though they may not be aware of number vibrations, feel they cannot settle on a name for their child until after the baby has been born.)

For parents naming their child in the 21st century, there is plenty of scope. There are fewer numbers filling the birthdate chart than in earlier centuries, leaving extra spaces to be filled by the numbers relating to the name.

Let's choose a name for a baby girl born on 21/9/2007. Her ruling number is $2 + 1 + 9 + 2 + 7 = 21 = 3$. Her day number is $2 + 1 = 3$.

Here is her birthdate chart:

		9
22		
1		7

We note that in this birthdate there are two isolated numbers, 7 and 9, and an empty centre column of the will (the arrow of frustration). Her ruling number and day number are both 3. To help balance out and strengthen this baby's vibrational field, we are looking for names that will fill the empty squares. The numbers missing from her birthdate chart are:

3	4	5	6	8
C	D	E	F	H
L	M	N	O	Q
U	V	W	X	Z

Filling the separation down the centre of the chart would be extremely helpful, and would help dilute the impact of the isolated numbers, 7 and 9. The vowels that offer us some of the missing numbers are A, E and O.

Let's try the name Chloe.

			6	5
C	H	L	O	E
3	8	3		

For Chloe, the soul urge is 6 + 5 = 11; the outer expression is 3 + 8 + 3 = 14 = 5; the name number is 11 + 5 = 16 = 7. All these help to expand upon and balance out the 3s in the ruling and day numbers.

Here is her name chart:

33	6	
	5	8

When we combine this baby girl's birthdate and name charts, we see that Chloe is a name that would significantly strengthen and balance her vibrational field:

Birthdate chart

		9
22		
1		7

Name chart

33	6	
	5	8

Combined chart

33	6	9
22	5	8
1		7

Chloe, born on 21/9/2007, now has the arrows of the planner, the arrow of the intellect, the arrow of emotional balance and the arrow of determination. Only one square on her combined chart is empty, and the isolated numbers of her birthdate chart are well diluted.

Even if she is sometimes known as or called Chlo, when we work it all out, we can see that the strength and balance remain, albeit slightly softened:

$$
\begin{array}{cccc}
 & & & 6 \\
C & H & L & O \\
3 & 8 & 3 &
\end{array}
$$

Soul urge number: 6
Outer expression: 3 + 8 + 3 = 14 = 5
Name number: 11

Birthdate chart

		9
22		
1		7

Name chart

33	6	
		8

Combined chart

33	6	9
22		8
1		7

For practice, and to show what a difference a name can make, let's try choosing a name for a baby boy born on the same day as Chloe. We'll try the name Jordon.

$$
\begin{array}{cccccc}
 & 6 & & & 6 & \\
J & O & R & D & O & N \\
1 & & 9 & 4 & & 5 \\
\end{array}
$$

For Jordon, the soul urge is $6 + 6 = 12 = 3$; the outer expression is $1 + 9 + 4 + 5 = 19 = 10$; the name number is $3 + 10 = 13 = 4$. Jordon's soul urge reinforces the 3s in his ruling and day numbers while the 10 and 4 help to balance them out.

Here is his name chart:

	66	9
	5	
1	4	

The name Jordon gives the arrow of determination and the arrow of the will, and dilutes the isolated numbers 7 and 9 from the birthdate chart.

When we combine this baby boy's birthdate and name charts, we see that Jordon is a name that significantly strengthens and balances his vibrational field:

Birthdate chart		
		9
22		
1		7

Name chart		
	66	9
	5	
1	4	

Combined chart		
	66	99
22	5	
11	4	7

Jordon, born on 21/9/2007, now has the arrow of practicality, the arrow of the determination, the arrow of emotional balance and the arrow of the will. Only two squares on his combined chart are empty, and the isolated numbers of his birthdate chart are well diluted.

However, if Jordon is sometimes known as or called Jordi, when we work it all out, we introduce the arrow of hypersensitivity to his name chart and significantly alter his name numbers:

$$6 \qquad\qquad 9$$
$$J \quad O \quad R \quad D \quad I$$
$$1 \qquad\quad 9 \quad 4$$

Soul urge number: 6 + 9 = 15 = 6
Outer expression: 1 + 9 + 4 = 14 = 5
Name number: 6 + 5 = 11

When we look at the combined chart for Jordi, although it still offers a reasonable balance, we can see that it will be preferable to call this boy Jordon most of the time.

Birthdate chart		
		9
22		
1		7

Name chart		
	6	99
1	4	

Combined chart		
	6	999
22		
11	4	7

CHANGING NAMES

Being called by a name we don't like, or by too many different names, can be very unsettling. The vibration of our name bombards us every day, so we are well-advised to use only a name or names with which we feel happy and compatible. Some people prefer their nickname; others prefer the full name given to them at birth, and will insist that it not be shortened. Children have even been known to refuse to respond to a name they truly dislike, until their parents relent and change it to something harmonious.

Consider this scenario: Roslyn dislikes being called Ros, and her wishes are respected by family and friends. Someone Roslyn barely knows begins calling her Ros. It grates so much on her that she asks the person to call her by her full name. The vibration of 'Ros' actually assaults her energetically.

If a person is genuinely unhappy or uncomfortable with the name they are being called, it may serve them well to examine their name chart in combination with their birthdate chart to see what the vibrational issues are.

Here is an example of a woman, born on 14/5/1950, whose parents named her Elizabeth, and who has always been called by her full name. Her birthdate totals 25 which gives her a ruling number of 7. Her day number (1 + 4) is 5. Her birthdate chart looks like this:

		9
	55	
11	4	

Here are the numbers for her everyday name:

```
5        9       1        5
E    L   I   Z   A   B    E   T   H
     3       8       2        2   8
```

Her soul urge is 20 = 2; outer expression is 23 = 5; and everyday name number is 2 + 5 = 7.

The name chart for Elizabeth looks like this:

3		9
22	55	88
1		

So Elizabeth, with a strong ruling number of 7, has been grappling for many years with the impact of an equally strong name number of 7 as well. Her combined birthdate and number charts look like this:

3		99
22	5555	88
111	4	

This woman's soul urge of 2, as well as the very full soul plane of the combined chart, and the two 7s — ruling number and name number — are extremely taxing.

For the sake of her health and happiness, she would be well advised to consider changing her name to something more harmonious with her birthdate.

The empty squares on her birthdate chart are 2, 3, 6, 7 and 8. So she should begin by looking for names with letters that fill those squares. Many possible names seem to contain 5s, and she already has two of those in her birthdate. Let's consider Jodi, which is a name she feels comfortable with; it also has the positive initial vowel, O.

```
        6       9
    J   O   D   I
    1       4
```

This would give her a soul urge of 15 = 6; an outer expression of 5; and an everyday name number of 11.

Her combined birthdate and name charts will now look like this:

	6	99
	55	
111	44	

If Elizabeth decides to change her name to Jodi, she is likely to feel a real sense of comfort and relief. Her overall chart is better balanced and now has the arrow of will as well as the arrow of determination.

Her new soul urge of 6 will support creativity as well as a love of home and family. The outer expression number 5 will bring freedom and fun into her life. And her everyday name number of 11 enhances spirituality as well as complementing her ruling number of 7.

DESTINY NUMBER

Your destiny number represents your place in the world. It is found by adding the numbers of all the letters in the name you were given at birth.

CALCULATING THE DESTINY NUMBER

It is important to calculate the value of each name because the first name represents personal attitude and feeling; the second name represents the reservoir from which power can be drawn; and the third or surname brings with it family characteristics.

Here is an example:

```
M  A  R  Y     E  L  L  E  N     J  O  N  E  S
4  1  9  7     5  3  3  5  5     1  6  5  5  1
   21              21               18
    3     +        3     +          9      = 15 = 6
```

Mary Ellen Jones's destiny number is 6.

Her personal attitude and feeling resonate to 3; the reservoir from which she draws her power also resonates to 3; and her family characteristics resonate to the vibration of 9.

MEANINGS OF DESTINY NUMBERS

Allied to, but broader and more sweeping in scope and scale than your ruling number, your destiny number offers a vision of your potential, should you choose to follow your most harmonious purpose and path in life.

NUMBER 2 DESTINY

Your role in life is one of peacemaker. Goodwill towards others is the energy and attitude that powers success for you. You are one of life's 'trouble-shooters' and will be called upon constantly to pour oil on troubled waters. You have a mission to fulfil, not only for the sake of success but also for your own peace and happiness.

Partnerships are important to you. No matter how independent you are, co-operation is essential to your success. Sharing is a means to your own attainment. You have the ability to influence people, you are sensitive and should appreciate how others feel. Your understanding and persuasive manner give you the ability to encourage and comfort people.

NUMBER 3 DESTINY

You have a creative destiny and are required to be the optimist. Your mission is to help people realise the magic power of cheerfulness and inspiration. Many people have lost the joy of living and it is your duty to arouse their imagination and spirit, and to help them laugh again. This may not always be easy for you but this is a part of your success and you should make every effort to live up to it. Mix with people who have a constructive philosophy when things go wrong.

NUMBER 4 DESTINY

Your destiny is to play the role of the manager and organiser. You are a builder and it is your mission to make things permanent and lasting. You must make dreams practical and bring all imagination down to earth. Life will not allow you to take things easy and you may meet many problems until you become proficient in establishing systems, order, form and regulation in your business and personal affairs. You may not always want to do this but if you wish to draw the best from life, you must always endeavour to establish an acceptance of responsibility.

NUMBER 5 DESTINY

Your mission offers many changes and experiences and represents freedom and progress. The meaning of the word 'freedom' here does not mean you should break convention or be rebellious. Instead, utilise your capacity for freedom to be a lawmaker, with charity and tolerance. You will find opportunity through people.

You usually have too many projects going at the same time, which scatters your energy/forces, so take heed and guard against this failing.

NUMBER 6 DESTINY

Your destiny is one of service and comforting those who are weak and unhappy. Duty will follow you inside and outside of the home, but your happiness will depend on the good you do for others. You must not confuse your duty with sacrifice. Keep truth and justice in the hearts and minds of yourself and others, and do not forget that you include the role of teacher in your destiny. Give to others and you will find yourself surrounded by love and comfort.

NUMBER 7 DESTINY
Your destiny is that of teacher. You never stop searching for knowledge and your life should be interesting. You will discover many hidden truths and make unusual associations in your search. It is your destiny to counsel and advise, so do not feel alone and always remember that as an educator you may not have an easy pathway. It will be through your knowledge, science and wisdom that you find your rightful place.

Guard against excessive emotion or sentiment because others are guided by your tolerance. You will be loved and respected for what you attain.

NUMBER 8 DESTINY
Your destiny is referred to as a 'dynamic destiny'. Your life will not be easy but you will have the right to position and money. Always remember this: a quest for *money only* will not bring you success. Your goal is to combine and balance material and spiritual laws, putting the law of cause and effect into operation, before any lasting reward can be achieved.

NUMBER 9 DESTINY

This is the pathway of the humanitarian and all that is charitable and beautiful. Your opportunities are many and a full return is achieved, but you must give love, tolerance, compassion, understanding and generosity to others. One of the greatest lessons is to offer forgiveness to all and to always use your power for the good of humanity.

Look for the beautiful — not the sorrowful — in life so that you can be true to your destiny of love and service to others.

NUMBER 10 DESTINY

This brings leadership through your own initiative and independence. Your life is destined to be interesting, with many odd and strange experiences. Success will come through your ability to stand on your own feet and remember that life will never let you down if you use your power constructively.

NUMBERS 11 AND 22 DESTINIES

The destiny pathway for these people can encompass the full cycle of experiences. The number 11 has the number 2 destiny — peacemaker and trouble-shooter — *intensified*. 11 is often referred to as the spiritual messenger.

The number 22 has the number 4 destiny — manager, organiser, builder — *intensified*. 22 is often called the spiritual master in form.

NUMBER 33/6 DESTINY

Your destiny brings leadership and inspiration and is referred to as the Master Teacher. You are meant to inspire by speech and deed.

FIRST AND LAST LETTERS OF A NAME

The first letter of a name gives the clue to the positive character of the name. It is written, 'The heart of the master is where we enter.' The entrance into your name is an open door to mastery in the manner specified by that letter. Where and how we enter is our registration for self-attainment.

The last letter of our name indicates the vibration we will have achieved when we have lived all the experiences our name can bring to us.

It is believed that Pythagoras, in the latter stage of his life, changed his name after many initiations and was called Yarancharya. He used the letter Y, which he considered very mystical, and although the Y vibrates to the number 7 (sacrifice), it is also a physical number, meaning 'the teacher'. The name ends with A and relates to the personal earth number 1, opening all doors of knowledge.

Here is another example: the name, Howard (used as a first name).

The first letter, H, vibrates to the number 8 which means this man is likely to approach life independently, to be comfortable in the corporate or business arenas, and to have a focus on money-making.

The last letter, D, resonating to 4, indicates that even when Howard has learned all that the 8 vibration has to teach him, he will still be a no-nonsense practical kind of person, and one who has achieved stability in his life.

If Howard chooses to be called Howie, changing the last letter of his name to an E which vibrates to 5, his approach to life will remain the same but is likely to lead to a sense of freedom which might include the capacity for practical inventions.

THE NUMEROLOGY OF SOME COMMON WORDS

It is not generally recognised that all words resonate to the vibrations of their numbers. Exploring the vibrational qualities of words can deepen our understanding of their true meanings.

Consider the word 'woman'. The vowels O and A resonate to the numbers 6 and 1 and show a soul urge of 7, indicating that woman has a capacity and an urge to help and to teach, as well as having inner strength and endurance. The consonants W, M and N resonate to 5, 4 and 5, totalling 14/5 and reflecting an outer expression that is both practical and flexible. 5 plus 7 gives a word vibration of 1 + 2 = 3, which has the same impact as a ruling number 3: optimistic, expressive, capable.

The chart for 'woman' clearly shows inner strength:

	6	
	55	
1	4	

If we look at the word 'mother', we find a soul urge of 6 (O) plus 5 (E) totalling 11, which indicates spiritual awareness and understanding. The outer expression of 4 (M) plus 2 (T) plus 8 (H) plus 9 (R) equals 2 + 3 = 5, reflecting creativity and a fun-loving nature. The total word vibrates to 11 + 5 = 16 = 7, indicating the sacrifices required of mothers.

Here is the chart for 'mother':

	6	9
2	5	8
	4	

The word 'mother' resonates with wisdom, discernment, and the ability to understand and guide, but only through deep, unselfish love can the word 'mother' be truly lived.

It is interesting to compare the values of the words 'father' and 'mother'.

The soul urge of 'father' is 1 + 5 which totals 6 — creative mind and strength of the man expressed in the home. The outer expression is 6 + 2 + 8 + 9 = 25; 2 + 5 = 7, indicating the strength and sacrifices fathers can be called upon to demonstrate. The total word vibrates to 6 + 7 = 13; 1 + 3 = 4, representing the hard-working stability and reliability so valued in fathers.

If the charts for 'mother' and 'father' are placed side by side, the only difference is that 'father' has a 1 on the earth plane while 'mother' has a 4. This reflects the traditional father role of provider, complemented by the support and understanding of the traditional 'mother'. Both of them are grounded, balanced, responsible, strong and stable.

Mother			Father		
	6	9		6	9
2	5	8	2	5	8
	4		1		

Another interesting example is the word 'love'.

```
      6     5
  L   O   V   E
  3       4
```

Soul urge is 11.
External expression is 7.
11 + 7 = 18 = 9.
Name number is 9.

The number 9 as a name number represents universal love and beauty. Note that the soul urge is the spiritual number 11.

Chapter 6

THE PYRAMIDS

I walked a mile with pleasure,
she chatted all the way,
but ne're a word I learned from her
for all she had to say.
I walked a mile with sorrow
and ne're a word said she,
but oh, the things I learned from her
when sorrow walked with me.

'ALONG THE ROAD', THOMAS BROWNING HAMILTON

The pyramids show influences at certain ages. Because we have the element of choice, we can use the positive or negative approach; it is up to each of us. And knowing the prevailing influences of each period of one's life can assist us in making wise and constructive choices.

This chapter explains how to chart the peaks, determine at what age each one occurs, and plot the numbers that vibrate to influence each period. Before we go into detail, let's look at the general principles involved.

There are four peaks. The first three peaks each have a nine-year duration, occurring during a period of 27 years which begins in each person's late 20s or early 30s. Within each nine-year cycle, we can experience a dormant period during the PYNs 4 and 5 and a mini-peak in the PYN 6. When we reach a peak, our PYN is always 9.

The number vibration on the fourth and final peak remains with us for the rest of our lives.

HOW TO SET UP A PYRAMID CHART

There are several steps involved in drawing up a pyramid chart. This method is simple if you follow the directions precisely and carefully. Use the birthdate example given, checking against the diagrams provided. Keep practising until the technique and method fall into place.

Example birthdate: 13/7/1974

Ruling number = 5

Draw a pyramid chart like this:

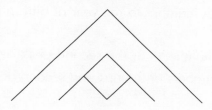

Place the **month** of the birthdate to the left at the base of the pyramid as shown (always reduce to single numbers). In this case, the month number at the base of the pyramid is 7.

Place the **day** of the birthdate in the centre at the base of the pyramid as shown (always reduce to single numbers). In this case, 13 (1 + 3) = 4, so the day number at the base of the pyramid is 4.

Add the digits of the **year** of the birthdate (1 + 9 + 7 + 4) = 21 (1 + 2) = 3, and place this single digit of 3 (the year number) on the right at the base of the pyramid.

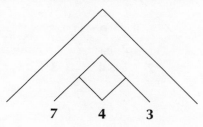

7   4   3

Next, to obtain the numbers for the pyramid peaks:

Add the month number to the day number: 4 + 7 = 11. Reduce this number to 2.

Place the number 2 at the first peak.

Add the day number to the year of birth number: 4 + 3 = 7.

Place the number 7 at the second peak.

Add the numbers of the first and second peaks together: 2 + 7 = 9.

Place the number 9 at the third peak.

Add the month number and year of birth number together: 7 + 3 = 10.

Place the number 10 at the fourth peak.

Note *that the numbers 10 and 11 are only written at the third and fourth peaks. If numbers add to 10 or 11 for the first and second peaks, these numbers are reduced to 1 and 2.*

So, we now have the numbers for the four peaks, namely: 2, 7, 9, 10.

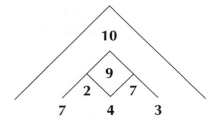

Next, to obtain the age of the person at the first peak:

ALWAYS begin with the mystical number of **36** (in ancient times, 36 was called 'the number of Man'). This ensures that each person is under a 9 personal year number when reaching a pyramid peak.

SUBTRACT the ruling number of the person (in this case, ruling number 5) from 36.

The answer is 31.

So this person will be 31 years of age on their first peak.

To obtain the ages for this person at the second, third and fourth peaks:

Add 9 to 31 = 40 (age at second peak).

Add 9 to 40 = 49 (age at third peak).

Add 9 to 49 = 58 (age at fourth peak).

(The 9s are added because there are 9 years between each peak.)

Summing up, the ages on each of the peaks of this person's pyramid chart are: 31, 40, 49, 58.

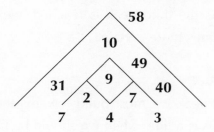

THE MEANINGS OF THE NUMBERS ON THE PEAKS OF THE PYRAMIDS

To gain the best from each of these nine-year periods, we must adapt to each vibration. Some people will resist adapting, and fight the vibration if it has a negative feel; but this is unwise, as resistance will only help to ensure that things go wrong. This is always the case when we resist or fight vibrational flow.

THE FIRST PEAK

This usually applies to the self. It is a time of realisation. As we journey to the second peak, those nine years can be rather trying.

THE SECOND PEAK

On the second peak, a period of obligation to other people and other things arises. This is a testing time of responsibility and family. As the third peak is reached, we usually find that life becomes more certain.

THE THIRD PEAK

On this third peak we must build towards the fourth and final peak. This is a time when we should be firmly placed, as the position or state in which we arrive at the fourth peak tends to dominate our remaining years as far as earthly progress or changes are concerned. If our lives have not been steadily built towards security and protection, we may experience loneliness and unhappiness.

THE FOURTH PEAK
By the time the fourth peak is reached, we should have achieved a reasonable level of wisdom and understanding. It is by no means a signal for departure from this life, but any serious illness at this time is more difficult to overcome. Also at this time, material losses are rarely regained.

NUMBER 1 ON THE PEAK
This is the number of individuality and leadership. There will be a strong desire to stand alone, face life and make progress. If 1 appears on the first peak, life can be difficult because of lack of experience. Sometimes the young person resists direction. In this case, a study of the name vibration may help. Under this vibration domestic mistakes are made, but not purposely. They need to be persuaded to go on a holiday — take a break. Try to be patient with them.

On any peak, the number 1 forces the person to stand up to life and think.

NUMBER 2 ON THE PEAK
This number stands for partnerships and always brings others into the equation. This is not an independent period, but one in which to develop harmonious relationships with

NUMEROLOGY

others. The key words during this vibration are co-operation, listening and understanding.

The number 2 on the first peak brings difficulties because the person is inclined to be too sensitive, and finds situations difficult to handle.

All peaks with the number 2 carry the lesson of co-operation. Difficulties in partnerships and friendships occur. Personal hurts and sometimes divorce happens if co-operation is not cultivated. If the addition of the peak adds to an 11 (1 + 1= 2) on the first or second peak, the main lesson is in spiritual thinking and faith.

Very often under this vibration, there are two pathways opening up. The best approach is to follow your own intuition, particularly if the number on the next peak is rising.

Rewards of the number 2 peak come through deeper understanding of others and unusual lines of activity or production. However, if emotions are not kept in check, rewards are unlikely to eventuate.

NUMBER 3 ON THE PEAK

This is the number of inspiration and artistic achievement. Generally it is an easy peak and deals with feelings. It brings opportunities through writing and speaking and gives the pleasures of life. It also carries an attraction for money.

With a number 3 on the first peak, a young person can waste life and generally does not want to work, looking only for enjoyment. This can cause regrets later.

On the second and third peak, a number 3 working with education can reap wonderful results.

The number 3 is a mind number and gives strength. Under this influence big decisions can be made, which may be beneficial. This number also invites travel.

In most cases, the 3 influence brings sorrow of some kind.

NUMBER 4 ON THE PEAK

When a number 4 is on the first peak, it means the person will be serious and practical. As a general rule, a number 4 on any peak lays a good foundation for the future. This is the number of order, system and endeavour and is usually hard working, with some economic problems and a responsibility to others. Under this influence a person can manage and organise. However, the number 4 peaks need maturity of mind and can be a difficult time if the positive side to this number is not observed.

Wise decisions will be made under its influence. It is a solid number — it indicates a time to build and plan. Progress may be slow but it is sure.

Health must always be watched under this influence.

NUMBER 5 ON THE PEAK

This will bring activity and the unexpected. This is never a
settled condition, but it brings a feeling of freedom. This
number brings opportunities but care should be taken not
to act too hastily. Under this vibration great progress and
big decisions can be made. Whether they are right or wrong
is entirely up to the person.

The number 5 stands for progress and advancement if
the positive is observed. As far as financial status is
concerned, it represents uncertainty, yet money seems
available when needed.

On a first peak the young person is bound to be restless
and make changes before waiting for results of their labour.

On the second and third peaks, the number 5 represents
great freedom, especially if it follows a 6 or 4; and this can
be a very happy time of life. Always carefully study any
legal documents as quarrels and legal affairs can bring
problems.

On a fourth or final peak, it again represents freedom
and activity, but it is important to avoid impulsiveness.

NUMBER 6 ON THE PEAK

On the first peak this vibration can bring duty to home and
responsibilities to family. It also brings love and protection
through that same family. Sometimes this duty to family can
last longer than the first peak, unless a 5 or 7 is on the next
peak. A 6 on any peak can represent duty and responsibility.

If the person does not accept this responsibility then reward or satisfaction will not be forthcoming.

This vibration brings all kinds of home changes such as moving, buying, selling, renovations, coming into the home or going out of the home. If the opportunity arose, it would be a successful time to go into public life or business.

This is a humanitarian number and the person under its vibration is meant to bring comfort to many people.

On a final fourth peak the duty can pay dividends, giving worthwhile recognition. Many people marry or have a lasting partnership at this later stage of life and are very happy. On this final peak and after much wisdom has been gained, it indicates a happy and useful older age.

NUMBER 7 ON THE PEAK

All number 7 peaks represent soul development. It is a time of testing and it represents knowledge and understanding. Education and scientific interests should be cultivated. It is the number of perfection and demands the best, but it is also proud, exclusive and something of a separatist.

When a 7 is on the first peak, it often brings a repression in some way — possibly lack of money for education, very strict parents or poor health.

This vibration represents study and specialising. But a misunderstood person who is under this vibration can bring problems in the family. Negative moods can defeat the purpose of this 7 peak.

A 7 peak is the time to study and specialise, and to work to a deeper understanding of what life is all about. Knowledge and skill under this vibration can bring success and money. But guard against restlessness and seeking the grass on the other side of the fence.

A 7 on any pinnacle demands truth and right living. When knowledge, understanding and training have been obtained, a 7 peak brings fine rewards and the power to attract all things.

NUMBER 8 ON THE PEAK

This represents strength, courage, ambition, authority and enterprise. It's a time for business expansion and often brings new ideas. Generally, it won't depart from business. It also represents attainment through endeavour.

During this vibration, business, property and professional activities are evident. It is not an easy peak because it demands intelligence to be applied. During an 8 peak, if lived constructively, possessions, property and success are available. To obtain these things it is often found that money needs careful managing and sometimes family and relatives will need supporting. Do not trust to luck. Use your knowledge and understanding.

The influence of the 8 brings a strong desire to be independent.

On all 8 peaks there is an opportunity to be a VIP in a small or large way.

NUMBER 9 ON THE PEAK

The number 9 represents colour, beauty and art. It brings tolerance, compassion and love. The number 9 is not an easy peak unless these qualities are well developed. By the time the 9 peak has been completed, tolerance and compassion must be learned to avoid great disappointment. This number represents all people and all religions. It brings added responsibility.

Travel and a full life will reward those under this vibration if the higher principles are expressed; otherwise this can be an unhappy time.

When 9 is on the first peak, a love affair, marriage or a line of work may be completed and left behind. This can be a blessing.

There may be changes affecting you, caused by someone else.

During the second and third peaks, there will be emotional experiences. To forget the 'self' is the lesson here, which then brings tolerance and understanding.

Money can be made and lost and just as easily won again.

This is not a helpful time to recover from serious illness.

NUMBER 10 ON THE PEAK

This number is found only on the third or fourth peak. As this is the number of individuality and leadership, it makes the person stand on their own feet and progress. This number creates restlessness and is a time for changes. Maybe it's a change of job or moving. It also can mean travelling.

If a 10 on the third peak is followed by a much lower number on the fourth peak, the nature of the change during the time at the third peak can be tumultuous and extreme.

As a final fourth peak, 10 is often a release to work on personal ideas developed during the other peak periods.

Number 10 peaks are never easy and will demand courage.

Do not over-extend yourself and be aware that this is a nervy vibration.

NUMBER 11 ON THE PEAK

This number is found only on the third and fourth peaks. This vibration strengthens spiritual desires, but can often scatter the nerves leading to general upheaval.

As the number 11 is the number of spiritual guidance and carries extremes in conditions, it could bring many varied experiences.

If the person is living to the true meaning of the number there will be triumph over adversities and the evolvement of a deeper self. On the other hand, if you live for material experiences only, you could bring about worrying conditions causing the nerves to shatter.

If the number 11 is on the third peak and the fourth peak is followed by a much lower number, the upheaval could be serious.

Chapter 7

MAKING MAJOR
LIFE DECISIONS

*People speak of lucky numbers. There is no such thing
as luck. Numbers reveal certain powers and tendencies,
but each individual must take advantage of their
opportunities and do their part in achieving any real
success in life. People who are enlightened by the science
of numbers know their strengths and weaknesses and
the times, favourable and unfavourable, that will occur.
They can shape and live their lives intelligently.*

NUMBERS AND THEIR INFLUENCE, HETTIE TEMPLETON

In this chapter, we will examine how you can use your understanding of numerology to assist you in making decisions in many of life's key areas: relationships, parenting, career, real estate, business, travel.

In reality, we are making decisions on the run many times a day, every day of our lives. That is part of being human: we all have free will and choice. Ultimately, whatever choice we make will teach us valuable life lessons. Always, the responsibility for our decisions lies squarely with us; the numbers merely serve as useful guides.

Throughout our lives, there will be favourable times and unfavourable times for different kinds of activities. Personal year numbers give a good indication as to which years favour relationships, change, money matters and so on. Examining our unique set of numbers helps us discern how that information applies specifically to us and how well equipped we are to work with different prevailing influences.

To begin the process, scan through the following pages and read whatever specific information is relevant to the decision you are considering at the moment.

Next, take a large sheet of paper on which you set up your birthdate chart, your name chart, your ruling number, day number, personal year number and your pyramid chart showing where you are with regard to peaks and their influences.

Now, take a deep, long look at all aspects of your overall and current personal influences. Refer to the relevant information and examples throughout this book to ensure that you have gleaned a balanced comprehensive reading. Remember to consider what part of a 9-year cycle you are in: are the numbers rising to a peak? Falling from a peak? What are the numbers on this peak and the ones before and after it?

When you feel you have examined everything as thoroughly as possible, put it all together in your mind or on paper and apply the insights to your decision-making process. By this stage, you will probably have an intuitive sense or feeling about what decision is likely to engender a positive outcome.

An important point to remember: unless you are acting alone, *always* consult with your partner or partners (business or personal). Consider the numbers for each person involved in the situation. Look particularly at each set of personal year numbers. Where applicable, look at the pyramid charts to see whether numbers are rising or falling, and whether one of you is in a dormant period. Take time to talk everything over, then make your decision.

LOOKING FOR SOMEONE SPECIAL?

Some people always seem to be looking for someone. Why? Is it because of the way our society is structured, or perhaps because some of us feel happier being with others? Whatever the individual reasons, humans are sociable beings. Most of us will yearn for a companion or partner at some stage in our lives, so it is worth finding out which times offer us the best chance of meeting someone special.

What makes a relationship work? Not even the numbers can tell us that. There will be times when that special person comes along, but nothing happens. Then, months down the track, you meet up again. This time, things are different.

Sometimes we feel we have found that special person — but they don't seem to notice. On other occasions, someone is interested in you, but you have no desire to associate with him or her. Have you ever wondered why?

Well, perhaps the chemistry is just not there for one of you. On the other hand, perhaps you are not living your full potential. Have you looked after yourself in every way, including looking at your inner self? Are you wearing a happy face or a sad face? People are attracted to each other for so many reasons.

What our numbers — specifically, our personal year number — can show us are the periods most likely to favour the establishment or nurturing of a special relationship. The following list shows the relationship energy for each PYN, but it is a good idea to read the general information about your personal year number too, especially if it is the same as your ruling number.

PERSONAL YEAR NUMBER INFLUENCES ON RELATIONSHIPS

PYN 2   The focus in a 2 year is mainly on personal relationships.

PYN 3   A happy time when you could meet more than one special person.

PYN 4   Although this is usually a slow year, 4 is a partnership number so there are definitely possibilities.

PYN 5   You could meet that special person in a 5 year, but the relationship might not mature until the following year.

PYN 6   A romantic time, when love is in the air. Loving partnerships can flourish, but there is also the risk of thinking that a casual dalliance is something more.

PYN 7   Impulsiveness can lead to potentially painful mistakes in a 7 year.

PYN 8   Watch out for promiscuity. This year's focus on independence and money-making does not particularly favour relationships.

PYN 9   New love may be in the air. Say goodbye to the old love first.

PYN 10 If no romance is forthcoming, try taking up a sport or some other physical activity to distract your over-active mind.

PYN 11   Time to work out what is important. Perhaps
                there are some emotional problems to sort out
                before you attract the kind of partner you would
                like.

PYN 22/4   This year is similar to the personal year 4, but
                slightly different — because whatever happens,
                it could have been worse.

PYN 33/6   This is similar to the 6 personal year with some
                differences. Be patient and do not expect
                perfection from your partner. Do try to remember
                that nobody is perfect, including your dear self,
                and once you realise this you will feel much
                freer within yourself. Also, don't be afraid to
                show your partner the real you.

NUMEROLOGY AND PARENTING

Hettie Templeton had a particular passion for assisting parents
and children to live happily and healthily, and often focused
her numerology classes and teachings on parenting skills.

MONTH VIBRATIONS AND YOUR CHILD

She provided information on how the month of birth, and
its number vibration, influences a child's character and
personality, as well as specific characteristics of ruling

number influences on children (incorporated in the ruling number information given earlier in this book). The essence of Hettie's wisdom flows through this section.

JANUARY — 1
Children born in this month are very ambitious. They have a strong will, and do not respond well to force or restrictive directions. Their love of freedom can easily be mistaken for selfishness. Parents of January children need to understand this, and support their constructive initiatives.

FEBRUARY — 2
Children born in February tend to be timid or guarded, and can sometimes appear rebellious. They aim to achieve their desires quietly, yet can be all too easily set back at times. They have an inner strength which yearns for responsibility, although they do not readily impress anyone as being able to achieve their goals. If encouraged to come forward, they can develop confidence and self-esteem.

MARCH — 3
Children born in March have very strong mind power, keen imaginations and an inclination to want their own way at all costs. They are highly strung and must be reasoned with. They do not respond well to aggravation or ridicule but thrive on respect, patient understanding and support.

APRIL — 4

Those born in April are also strong yet often feel unhappy and suppressed. They are very willing to serve and, through small acts of service, can express themselves well and feel more content. They like to think for themselves and are decided in their views. A certain amount of freedom is essential for children born in April.

MAY — 5

Children born in May are unusually sensitive, and often struggle to maintain an appearance of equilibrium. If not understood, they can become very bad tempered and difficult to live with. Their loving natures blossom when they feel secure, understood and unrestricted.

JUNE — 6

Children born in June have a great inner longing to perform acts of service for those they love. But they also have an aloof way about them, which can easily turn to selfishness. They may exaggerate but it must be understood that this is because of the intensity of their feelings and their eagerness to make themselves understood. They like to be romantic.

JULY — 7

Children born in July seem to have their share of troubles in some direction or another, sometimes from ill health; but with loving support and their own great courage and fearlessness, they win through. They also have a wonderful capacity for understanding.

AUGUST — 8
Children born in August are very independent, preferring to carry out their own ideas and make their own decisions. Without a certain amount of freedom they will go to great lengths to get their own way, which often leads them into trouble.

SEPTEMBER — 9
Children born in September are very restless. They resent all kinds of discipline and thrive when they feel free to do their own thing. They often suffer from injustice through misunderstanding, and can become very stressed and oversensitive.

OCTOBER — 10
Although children born in October display a great love of freedom and pleasure, their motivation is not entirely selfish as they have deep understanding and an inner desire to please everybody. They resent interference with their plans and if thwarted they become very discouraged.

NOVEMBER — 11
Children born in November are very ambitious, always yearning to do something different from others. Their

ambition is often mistaken for rudeness, although this is furthest from their thoughts. They cannot be deceived, having a keen capacity for discernment. They also have a vivid imagination, which again often leads them into trouble but can also be a very positive resource.

DECEMBER — 3

Children born in December have a deep love of nature, which will only emerge when they feel loved and valued. They are not always easy to understand and can appear hard and disinterested, although they are not. They yearn to be loved and understood. Their desire to protect their loved ones is also very intense and often leads them into trouble.

WHEN SHOULD WE START A FAMILY?

Many people say that if a child is meant to come into this world, it will. No amount of planning or prevention is 100 per cent accurate or successful.

But if you are planning to get pregnant, along with all the practical considerations, there is some numerology work you can do. Calculate the personal year number for both yourself and your partner. PYNs that particularly support family expansion and the changes that come with babies are 5, 6, 8, 9 and 10. Their vibrational influences are listed on pages 91–94. Apply these insights to your considerations regarding future work options, income, care arrangements and partnership during the baby's early months and years.

Look at the list (above) of the characteristics of children born in particular months. You can aim for what you think you would like but, ultimately, whenever your baby is born will turn out to be the 'right' time.

RAISING YOUR CHILD

There are numerous excellent books devoted to child-raising, and I encourage you to read any and all that appeal to you.

Children whose parents truly understand them and give them loving personalised attention generally thrive. Drawing up your child's birthdate and name charts and studying them carefully, along with the influence of their ruling and day numbers, will give you invaluable insights to your child's strengths, challenges and predispositions. Pay particular attention to any arrows on each chart and on their combined birthdate and name chart.

Look also at your child's personal year number to help with making any significant decisions on your child's behalf. This can be very helpful if you are considering when to start your child at school, for example.

Many children born in the 21st century will have no 3, 6 or 9 on their birthdate chart. Especially if this has not been addressed by the numbers in their name, they come under the influence of the arrow of poor memory (see page

36). They will fare best if kept at home as long as possible. They may appear slow or backward when they do go to school, and complain of headaches. But parents who are aware of this will not be alarmed, knowing that by the age of about seven, this child will settle in and achieve just as well as others in the class.

Children need to be allowed to exercise their imaginations — by building things, in creative activities like painting, drawing and story-telling, and by thinking up new games to play or being imaginative when helping mum or dad.

They also need 'quiet time', especially at bedtime. Reading or being read to, or a quiet talk with mum or dad can settle their minds and help them to go to sleep easily and to sleep well.

Clear, firm guidance, understanding and unconditional love are wonderful parenting tools, no matter what influences may be around your child.

CONSIDERING A CAREER CHANGE?

Looking for a new career or looking to step up in your present job can be challenging, depending on how sensitive you feel. Some people enjoy the job they are in and stay in that job for many years — if they are competent and the boss likes them. Others are looking for promotion every year or so, and yet others may be seeking to better themselves outside the company.

Whatever the reason for leaving your present position, it's wise to calculate your personal year number and consult the following information before you make the leap.

PYN 2   Stay where you are for now. If you are already out of work and looking, be prepared for the vibrations to be fairly weak. If you happen to find yourself a job, you may not be happy and will have to begin the search again. Being accepted for a position at the end of this year, ready to begin a new job the following year, may be okay. What does your intuition say?

PYN 3   This is usually a happy year, and looking for a career change under these circumstances is a bit risky. It might be wise to count your blessings for now.

PYN 4   This is not a good time to change your career. Save as much as you can (which could be difficult) and sit tight.

PYN 5   If you feel the desire for change, have a holiday if possible. New work opportunities may arise. By all means, look around to see what is on offer.

PYN 6   The mini peak. Be prepared for whatever comes along. If you are in business, this is a good time to expand.

PYN 7   A year to consolidate. Not a good year for changes. Don't be too impulsive, as the result may be bitter-sweet.

PYN 8   Feeling restless? It might be time for a change if that's what you want. Otherwise, it may be time to look around or to step up in the company.

PYN 9   It's time to take up that new position — get rid of the old and get on with the new. If you are not looking for a new job, then your present one might have a few surprises for you.

PYN 10   Another year for opportunities. Put your best foot forward. Planning a long-term project? This is the year to do it.

PYN 11   Unless it's absolutely necessary, make no changes this year. Learn, and expand your knowledge.

PYN 22/4   Successful opportunities arise this year.

PYN 33/6   As referred to in the 6 personal year, this is a mini peak and, if in business, it is a good time to expand. If you are looking for a change, take note of where you are in life and whether a change is warranted. What does your intuition say? Go with that feeling.

MAKING IMPORTANT BUSINESS DECISIONS

If you decide to start a business, or sell or buy a property on your own (without a partner, business or otherwise), first work out what personal year you are in. It would *not* be wise to initiate a business venture in a personal year number 2, 3, 4, 7, 11 or 22/4 — although in a 22/4 PYN it might be possible.

In those years, it would be better to wait. Get all the background work done while you are waiting. For instance, you can save more money; research the market; look for a better location for your business or property. Don't just jump in.

If, on the other hand, you are offered a deal too good to refuse — then go ahead. The choice is always yours. Just remember to check your personal year number. If the timing is not right, it will take longer to get the business on its feet, and you can be prepared for that.

People buying a house or property in an unfavourable personal year often find that something goes wrong with the contract or that the other party opts out at the last minute. If you push against the tide, you might regret it when you realise that if you had waited another six months, a property that you much prefer would have been available.

Always carry out thorough practical searches and investigations when making any significant decision. It goes without saying that you will have an accountant closely examine the books of any business you consider buying. If your personal year number indicates it is a less than propitious time, take extra care: even a good accountant may not be sure that the books are honest.

When making business decisions with a partner (business or otherwise), look at the personal year number of that partner. If your partner is under the vibration of a 5, 6, 8, 9 or 10 year (and you are under the vibration of a 2, 3, 4, 7, 11 or 22/4) then the vibrational strength will come from your partner. (Remember it works round the other way as well.)

The following list shows the relationship of each personal year number to business dealings and buying and selling.

PYN 2   A year for coping with relationships, study, learning from life experiences. A research and planning year.

PYN 3   This is a happier, more carefree year. It is not a good time to make big decisions because an error is likely to happen while you are in such a light-hearted mood.

PYN 4   This is a preparation and consolidation time. A slow year. If you simply MUST make a decision — leave it till April/May or after August.

PYN 5   Busy and progressive. Check the fine print on contracts.

PYN 6   A good time to buy and sell a property or business, or to expand.

PYN 7   Not a good time to buy or sell. Consolidate. Think.

PYN 8   A good year for business and money-making. Be honest.

PYN 9   Be charitable in all your dealings and look for opportunities.

PYN 10   Decision-making time. Show personal strength. Money issues might arise. Under this influence you can set new goals and begin any long-term projects.

PYN 11   Be professional. You can continue to carry on with business.

PYN 22/4   This is a time somewhat like the 4, but is stronger.

PYN 33/6   As the 6 personal year under Business Decisions suggests, this is a good time to buy and sell property or business or to expand.

It is advised that you listen to your intuition because you are under a propitious time and you could be in a position to make a meaningful decision.

If you begin your business in a fortunate year, you can expect it to prosper. Bear in mind, of course, that all businesses are affected by market forces.

REAL ESTATE AND HOUSE NUMBERS

Whether you are planning to rent or buy, there are many practical and emotional factors to take into account. Most importantly, the place you choose as your home should meet your lifestyle requirements and make you feel happy and secure.

Keep in mind that the vibration of a house number is not in itself good or bad, positive or negative. Whether it will support you depends on the way it harmonises with the ruling number or numbers of the person or people who plan to live in the house. If you are on your own, working this out can be relatively simple. For a couple, a family or a group, it's not always that easy. Ultimately, after looking at what the house number represents, it is generally wisest to make your decision based on how everybody *feels* about the place and how well it meets all your needs.

CALCULATING HOUSE NUMBERS

To calculate the house number, add together all its components and reduce them to the lowest digit, ranging from 2 to 11. Do not reduce the 22/4. Any letters in the house number should be counted as their numerical equivalents, for example, 13B will be calculated as 1 + 3 + 2 = 6.

HOUSE NUMBER 2
This number can be a 2 or can add to 20 from multiple numbers.

If you have a dynamic personality, this house number may not suit. But if you are looking for some peace and quiet into which you can retreat after a busy day at work, then this might be the number for you. When a couple or family live in a 2 house, they must focus on being considerate and should be prepared to share.

HOUSE NUMBER 3
There will be some bright, happy times in this house and there will be people coming and going; this may be mixed with some sadness along the way.

In a 3 house, wittiness can be laced with criticism and this can become tiresome.

HOUSE NUMBER 4
This will be a no-nonsense house. The resident/s will most likely work hard or work long hours. It's a house that calls for plain speaking. Perhaps more spending than saving will be the order of the day. But plans can be made in this house.

HOUSE NUMBER 5
This house feels like a free lifestyle house. Although some discipline will be needed to make things happen, it can be done. A 5 house will provide the feeling of freedom that

supports activation of long-held plans, especially in any of the artistic forms.

HOUSE NUMBER 6
This house will have family responsibilities attached to it. It may be an unruly house if there are children, but it will be a house where love flows easily. Just as easily, though, it can all go in the opposite direction. It is, as usual, up to you.

HOUSE NUMBER 7
This will be a different household. It will be philosophical, sacrificial, but above all, it will be a house of learning and knowledge. Other people may be fascinated with its occupants.

HOUSE NUMBER 8
If there are children, this will be a house of either too much or not enough discipline. Money may be earned and saved. Life may appear hard, but ultimately worthwhile if the rules are adhered to.

If there are no children, this can be a corporate type of household, where residents are living and earning well. Those who live here will have worked hard for what they have and will show independence. But universal laws must still be obeyed.

HOUSE NUMBER 9
This is not a particularly easy house number as it will have responsibility attached to it. It may also be a household

where the occupants bring home lost animals or lost or troubled souls. This is a house where high ideals might be found or lost.

HOUSE NUMBER 10
This will be a house where adaptability is the key word. It will be proud but undemonstrative. People in this house may be well equipped to take care of themselves and work towards independence.

HOUSE NUMBER 11
This is a loving household if the inmates are happy. If not, caustic sarcasm will be prevalent.

11 is a spiritual number, so each resident must live up to their personal philosophy. Otherwise, conflicts will occur.

HOUSE NUMBER 22/4
This can be a household of obstinate silence or silent understanding. It is not an easy number but it can generate wonderful revelations. It is either very strong or very weak.

HOUSE NUMBER 33/6
There could be a mixture of love and conflict in this house, but with some lively debates.

Some might consider that money is important, while others consider feelings and how we treat others are very important. Then there will be those who consider that both are important.

Now the decision is yours. But as stated earlier, it is often the *feel* of a house rather than the influence of the house number that is most important. The number does have some effect, but with awareness, we can adjust our attitudes and behaviours to focus on the positives in most life situations.

ANYONE FOR TRAVEL?

Many factors affect our decisions to travel. Some situations offer us more choice of travel times than others. If you have the opportunity to choose the most favourable times, look carefully at the personal year number details that follow and review them in conjunction with your ruling number. If you have a travelling companion, check out their numbers too, remembering that the stronger vibrations will carry the weaker vibrations. It's best for the person with the stronger vibrations to make all the arrangements if that's possible. It might be that the person with the stronger personal year vibrations will have a happier time and you will make the best of it. But being together is what it's about, isn't it?

Even those who travel a lot in their job will enjoy it more at some times than at others. Understanding the influences can make this easier to handle.

PYN 2   There will be a few personal hurts and it would be better to travel at another time. If you travel for study or learning purposes, with or without expenses paid, you will learn a lot because PYN 2 governs study and learning.

If you are a ruling number 2 person, travelling in this year could be taxing on your health. There may also be disappointments with a person or some issue.

PYN 3   Travelling under this vibration sounds good and feels right, but give it some thought. If someone close to you is not well and you are away, you may feel bad about that. Otherwise, it could be a good and happy time.

If you are a ruling number 3 person there may be a lot going on in your life. It would be a good idea to take vitamin supplements that strengthen the nervous system.

PYN 4   If you have travel plans for the first half of this year, there may be a few setbacks. If you insist on travelling this year, perhaps you could wait till after April — see how that feels. After August would be even better. Money may not exactly be flowing into your pockets so keep an eye on your finances. This is also another time to be careful of your health.

If you are a ruling number 4 person, travel may not be possible this year — unless it is with work. This is a limiting time for you.

PYN 5   Oh what a feeling, after the previous year. There should be new situations, places and people: everything travel has to offer.

If you are a ruling number 5 person, you will feel that you have so much freedom. This is not always a good thing because there may be situations where you could easily overstep the line.

PYN 6   Love is in the air and you might well follow it with travel. If you're already travelling, you may find it in several places, several times. This can be a good time for meeting people and having happy times. Perhaps you might even want to come home and settle down.

If you are a ruling number 6 person, there may be too much responsibility at home for you to travel at this time.

PYN 7   Unless your travel includes study or learning experiences, it would be best not to go. This is a year when impulsiveness strikes and we sometimes talk ourselves into a situation that may not be the best for us.

If you are a ruling number 7 person and you decide to travel, you may end up with little or no money. It might have been an impulsive decision to travel.

PYN 8   Travel for business is supported at this time. If you want to travel for pleasure and you're feeling courageous, then do it. Follow your intuition. But remember, this could be a difficult year. 8 is ruled by the planet Saturn, so always tell the truth.

If you are a ruling number 8 person, you may experience some financial strain, so consider this before you travel.

PYN 9   This seems like a good travelling time for most people. If you are in the older age group, perhaps you have retired and now wish to do a bit of travel. Good for you.

If you are a ruling number 9 person, there will be some sacrifice you might have to make. There will be a good deal of emotional strain so you must watch your health. Because of these things, it may be wise for you not to travel. You know your life: think about the circumstances and take it from there.

PYN 10   Travelling under this vibration seems good. Make your own decision here. It will probably be a big year for changes one way or another — you might even make some extra cash. So it is up to you.

If you are a ruling number 10, you might be unsettled and be in two minds about many things. If you decide to travel, it might be better to go on your own, but here again, it is up to you.

PYN 11   It's not a good idea to rush into any travel plans under this vibration — but if you have to, you have to. It might be better to face up to family problems. Then again, the lessons you learn in your travels may be just as valuable as facing up to those issues at home.

If you are a ruling number 11, consider whether certain issues are upsetting your nerves and brain power. Under these circumstances, if you wanted to get away from it all for a while, travelling might be the thing. But think before you leap.

PYN 22/4 If you are living your life selfishly, this strong master number can be destructive. On the other hand, if you're planning to travel to Somalia or Ethiopia to do kindness for the betterment of the human race, then all will go well for you. This vibration can bring successful opportunities in your everyday life, so think carefully where you would travel to do the most good. Otherwise, stay at home and do good things.

If you are a ruling number 22/4, you could be in for a personal shock, so if you are travelling abroad (or even if you are not), be prepared.

PYN 33/6 As the 6 personal year under Travel suggests, this is a good time to meet people and communicate with them. If you are travelling for business reasons you should do well.

Perhaps you are travelling in a teaching capacity and, if so, you will get your point across beautifully. So long as you do not expect people to be perfect, this should be a bright and happy time.

If you are looking for that special person, you could well draw that person to you in this particular year.

No matter what the reason for your travel, your inspiration and intuition will be there for you and it is advised that you follow it.

MEDITATION AS A DECISION-MAKING TOOL

Meditating is a wonderful way of stilling the mind, making it easier to consider any decisions that might be pending. People who meditate regularly say that they feel calmer, more positive and more energetic.

There are many different kinds of meditation, all of them effective in their own way. Different styles suit different people.

The easy meditation described here is suitable for adults and for children. Children have a limited attention span, so in the beginning, a parent might sit with their child to read the meditation instructions to them and to help them with concentration and sitting still. Parents must decide when their child is old enough to engage in this exercise, but seven is generally a reasonable starting point. Before you introduce the meditation to your child, sit and talk quietly with them for a short time each day for a few days. If they find this difficult, perhaps they are not quite ready for meditation.

Whether you are learning to meditate yourself, or guiding your child, start with meditations of about five minutes duration, progressively extending the time to 10 minutes or more.

SIMPLE MEDITATION

Sit in a spot where you will be comfortable and not fidgety.

Close your eyes and relax.

Breathe deeply and evenly.

As you settle, your breathing will become shallower.

Try not to think of the happenings of the day or what you need to do tomorrow.

Now, imagine you are in a little boat drifting gently along a beautiful river.

There is nothing to harm you.

The day is sunny and warm and the sun is sparkling like jewels on the water.

You can see small birds flying above you and hear them twittering in the trees.

The grass on the riverbanks is a lovely green.

And the leaves on the trees have wonderful colours of green, red and yellow.

It is so very peaceful.

After a little while, bend your head slightly over the side of the boat and look deep into the water.

The water is crystal clear and you can see all the way to the bottom of the river.

Down there, you can also see smooth pebbles of all shapes and sizes.

There are small rainbow-coloured fish swimming about. Can you see them?

When you have finished looking into the water, sit back in the boat and relax.

Stay in that relaxed condition, drifting along in the boat, feeling the warmth of the sun, for as long as you can.

When you have finished, step out of the boat and feel the warm earth beneath your feet. Feel your body becoming solid and grounded.

Slowly open your eyes.

Chapter 8

SAMPLE CHARTS AND READINGS

Everyone has the obligation to ponder well
his own specific traits of character.

Cicero

The following charts are likely to provide fascinating insights into the accuracy of numerology in relation to well-known people. In addition, they offer serious students of numerology the opportunity to explore the subtleties and complexities of how a comprehensive chart and reading can be devised and presented.

Since this book was first published in 2007, I have added some further information about what is happening in the lives of these well-known people.

PAUL 'BONO' HEWSON,
MUSICIAN/ACTIVIST/PHILANTHROPIST
BIRTHDATE: 10/5/1960

Birthdate

Ruling number 22/4 (control issues; philanthropist).
Day number 10 (original, adaptable).
Arrow of determination 1, 5, 9 (strengthens determination to achieve).

Two numbers together: 6 and 9 on the mind plane (weighty responsibility).

Two 1s (sees both sides of things; rarely stuck for an answer).

PYN in 2006 was 5.

Bono has five empty squares in his birthdate chart. Clearly, his life indicates how much a person can achieve with a chart like this. But Bono does have strong numbers in his birthdate. He is a ruling number 22/4 and is born on a 10 day. The 22/4 gives him the ability to do whatever he decides he will do, and the 10 gives him that 'get up and go'. The arrow of determination adds further strength to this attribute. He shows originality, individuality, leadership, ambition and strong creativity — and all those qualities are supported by his day number of 10.

His ruling number 22/4 gives him many varied abilities, including that of philanthropist (22/4s are among the greatest philanthropists).

	1	3			6		6
P	A	U	L		B	O	N	O
7			3		2		5	

The name Paul has a soul urge of 4, an outer expression of 10 and a name number of 5. Bono has a soul urge of 3, an outer expression of 7 and a name number of 10.

Paul **Bono**

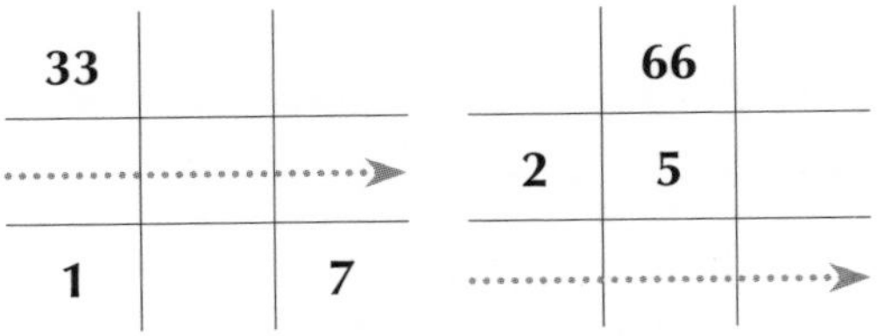

When young, he was generally uncontrollable and argumentative. The name 'Paul' did not suit him. He appeared to be a very confused lad. When we look at the name chart for 'Paul' we see that it has the arrow of hypersensitivity — no 2, 5, 8 — endowing him with daydream-like qualities and a sense of being misunderstood; it also predisposed him to misinterpret others. All the numbers add to a name number of 5, helping to scatter his forces and making him very nervy. This was opposing his ruling number of 22/4. He wanted to do everything and be everywhere. But what he really sought was clear direction for his energy.

In 1976 however, in his mid teens, he had the opportunity to form a band and became the lead singer. He had found music and, in doing so, had found himself. His life changed. He changed his name to Bono, a nickname given him by a school chum.

When the name 'Bono' is placed on a chart it gives him a 2, two 6s and a 5, and a name number of 10, which reinforces the originality and individuality given by his day number.

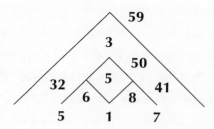

By the time he reached his first pyramid peak at 32 (a 6 peak), he was well on his way to becoming world renowned. In the years leading up to his second peak (an 8) he turned political activist, changed his image and emerged with his band to play a different sound. The words of his songs have 'taken people on spiritual journeys, turned them on sexually or inspired them to change.'

Now, beyond U2, Bono has extended himself to other projects and causes. From the year 2000 and to the present day he has devoted his time to playing on the world stage and crusading on behalf of the poor, speaking to politicians to help raise money or wipe a country's debt.

Bono is still under the influence of the 8 on his second pyramid. With his 22/4 ruling number, 10 day number and under the influence of 8 on the second pyramid peak, in a personal year number 6 in 2007, he still has plans in the pipeline.

Bono is still performing with U2 to rave crowds. The band was in Paris when terrorists struck on Friday 13th November 2015. Consequently they cancelled their scheduled shows (in Paris) for the 14th and 15th. Bono has many future plans for U2 with him still 'up front'.

At 55 years of age he will be under the vibrations of the number 5 on the third pinnacle and has been living through many varied experiences of contrasts. There is the number 3 on his fourth and final pinnacle, which indicates an overall happier life (with the usual unhappiness and sadness that we all experience).

Both the numbers on his third and fourth pinnacles indicate Bono will still continue performing with U2 and also raising money for many charities worldwide. He is a wonderful philanthropist, who personifies his ruling number, 22/4.

HILLARY CLINTON, FORMER FIRST LADY OF THE USA AND THE FIRST TO BE ELECTED TO THE UNITED STATES SENATE
BIRTHDATE: 26/10/1947

Birthdate

	6	9
2		
11	4	7 →

Ruling number 3 (plenty of personality).
Day number 8 (a corporate number).

Two numbers together: 6 and 9 on the mind plane (heavy responsibility).

Arrow of practicality and physicality 1, 4, 7 (practical; capable of being stern when necessary).

Two 1s (sees both sides of things; rarely stuck for an answer).

PYN in 2006 was 8.

Hillary Clinton appears to be a very matter-of-fact, down-to-earth person, supported by her arrow of practicality, day number 8 and the 6, 9 conjunction indicating responsibility. But through all of that, she can show a lighter side that comes from her ruling number 3.

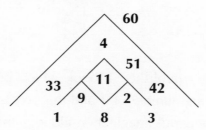

Hillary married Bill Clinton in 1975 before she reached the first peak on her pyramid, which is a 9. This number indicates that there may already have been some rocky moments in their married life together during that first peak and leading to the second peak. The vibration on the second peak is a 2 and during this time there would have been relationship issues to work through. This could have made or broken Hillary. But she chose to be strong and see her life through in her marriage.

As First Lady, Hillary was always controversial: she was never going to take a back seat (her solid earth plane, her day number and a ruling number that enjoys being in control, made sure of that).

	9			1		
H	I	L	L	A	R	Y
8		3	3		9	7

Hillary

33	↑	99
	⋮	8
1	⋮	7

In 1996 Hillary published a book which became a best seller. Her ruling number of 3 and the two 3s in her name give her a wonderful imagination along with the ability to write and to have her words sound interesting on the page.

Note that her name chart shows the arrow of action (7, 8, 9) and the arrow of frustration (empty 4, 5, 6). The numbers 4 and 6 on her birthdate chart somewhat dilute this empty arrow. Hillary's personal year number for 2006 was 8, indicating this would have been a difficult year for her (especially because her day number is 8). Even so, her personal graph is rising and she would be feeling the power of that 8. In 2007 she is under a personal year number of

9, reaching her fourth pyramid peak which is a 4. If Hillary plans to seek higher office, 2006, 2007 and 2008 would be good years in which to make a move. These are her power years at this time.

It is noted that Hillary's third peak exhibits an 11. The period between that third and fourth peak would have been another difficult time for her, especially in her private life. But the number 4 on that fourth peak in 2007 is a solid number indicating hard work. If Hillary utilises its positive influence, this number will lay the foundation for the rest of her life. Whatever has been ordained for her, she will not let up from doing what she does best — that is, work hard in whatever capacity she chooses. Hillary must also look after her health under this number.

Hillary has perhaps experienced some extreme events between the ages of 51 and 60 – and at 60 years on her fourth and final pinnacle of the pyramids is showing high results in the race for the United States Presidency. Hillary seems to be on the right track to obtain the top job. If her health stands up she's well on her way to becoming the first United States Woman President.

In 2015, under the influence of the 8, Hillary has been quite restless and putting up a strong fight for the Presidency.

In 2016 she is under the personal year number of 9, taking her to the end of one cycle and to the beginning of a new cycle. This has the 'look' of a new top job.

SHANE WARNE, CRICKETER
BIRTHDATE: 13/9/1969

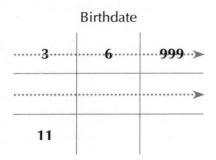

Ruling number 11 (understanding, but sometimes sarcastic).

Day number 4 (a good friend, but can be tough).

Arrow of the intellect 3, 6, 999 (sees things from a reasonably balanced point of view).

Arrow of hypersensitivity (no 2, 5, 8) (can be very touchy).

Two 1s (ability to speak his mind very quickly).

Three 9s (mental plane heavy — could have outbursts of temper).

PYN in 2006 was 3.

Shane Warne (Warnie) has a lot going for him — and a few things not going for him. His ruling number of 11 has been called the number of genius. This number 11 can be a nice number to live with and that day number 4 can be a good, solid friend. But we must look deeper. He has an empty arrow on the emotional plane (no 2, 5, 8), which can make him very touchy and also cause him to mistakenly take things personally. Shane has the mind plane filled (balanced) but those three 9s can give him a very bad temper. The two 1s give him a sharp tongue which, combined with his ruling number of 11, can make him sarcastic. So if things are not going his way, he has the ability to really let you know. If things are going his way, everything is right with him and the world, and a nicer bloke you wouldn't meet.

```
        1       5               1           9   5
  S   H   A   N   E       W   A   R   N   I   E
  1   8       5               5       9   5
```

Shane   **Warnie**

					99
	55	8		555	
11			1		

The names Shane and Warnie on a chart both give him numbers on the soul plane — the emotional plane — which helps balance out the arrow of hypersensitivity on his birthdate chart. Warnie also gives him the arrow of determination (1, 5, 9), and three 5s which indicate impulsiveness.

In 2006 Shane was under a PYN 3 influence. It was a happier year for him in many ways and also a sad time. He separated from his wife and children. But Shane found many new friends during this year, which also brought him certain realisations. In 2007 he will be under the influence of 4. This number will bring him down to earth in many ways. The number is a 22/4 which is stronger (more positive) than other numbers that add to 4. This 4 year might bring setbacks to Shane, but using his wisdom he can emerge in strength.

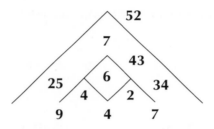

Looking now at his pyramids, we see that Shane was 34 when he reached his second peak, a 2. He will be under the influence of that 2 for approximately nine years, when he will reach his third peak, a 6. But until then he must learn about co-operation, consideration and relationships.

It has been said of Shane that he may well be one of the five best cricketers of all time. (This is where he shows his ruling number 11 genius.) He has also shown his philanthropic and spiritual side and displayed his emotions freely, giving material and physical assistance to the victims and children of the tsunami in Indonesia.

Shane is able to separate his private life from his professional life. He has things to learn in his private, personal relationships, while in his professional life, he finds he must 'toe the line' on many occasions.

Well, Shane is back on the cricket scene. It seems he's taken up the role of mentoring Australian spin bowlers in an official capacity and is in the front news of cricket again; also, along with his friend, the highly commended Indian batsman, Sachin Tendulka, Shane is currently promoting cricket to America. Well good luck with that, Warnie.

With Warnie's genius he just might win over the Americans – well hopefully some of them, anyway. In 2016 he is under the 4 personal year number. Under that vibration there'll be a few setbacks and some frustration, but that 4 might well lay a strong foundation for his efforts to bring the game to America. Shane is still under the influence of the number 6 on his pyramid, and if he keeps his 'cool' and a well-balanced outlook, his charm could win the day.

Perhaps there'll be some help from Tendulkar, who, in 2015 is under the influence of a personal year number 9 (a strong influence for change) and in 2016 is under the influence of the number 10, another strong number for pushing forward any project.

NICOLE KIDMAN, ACTRESS/BENEFACTOR
BIRTHDATE: 20/6/1967

Birthdate

	66	9
2		
1		7

Ruling number 4 (earth number; good solid friend; hard worker).

Day number 2 (first number on the soul plane; intuitive).

No arrows in chart (adaptable).

Two 6s and a 9 together on the mind plane (responsibility and worry in family and personal life).

One 1 on the earth plane (difficulty in speaking about personal self).

Isolated 7 on chart (repeated life lessons which can be painful until learned).

PYN in 2006 was 7.

Nicole feels comfortable with who she is. She is a good actress, a good ambassador and she clearly loves children. But no matter how comfortable we feel within ourselves, we all have trials, troubles and sacrifices, and Nicole is no exception. Within that isolated 7 she feels loneliness and deep emotions she cannot explain. Her acting takes her away from all of that while she is portraying 'someone else'. Eventually Nicole will overcome those negative feelings. She is an intelligent woman and will work it out for herself.

The two 6s on her birthdate chart indicate she will have lots of worry regarding her family circle and close friends. The 9 added to those 6s gives her responsibility, which may feel heavy at times. The 2 on the soul plane gives her intuitive ability, although she might not use it because of her ruling number 4. The 4 is a very practical, down-to-earth number, not given to intangible things. But if Nicole uses her wisdom, she will listen to that 'small voice' within.

```
        9          6          5
   N    I    C    O    L    E
   5         3         3
```

Nicole

```
·33·····6·····9·>
      55
····················>
```

Nic

```
   3    |    9
      5
·················>
```

Nicole's name chart reveals that the mind plane is filled and includes two 3s which give her the imagination, which may be lacking in her ruling number of 4. The two 5s in the name chart will, to some extent, dilute the isolated 7 on her birthdate chart, but they also stir up emotions that plague her and sometimes give her a 'sick' feeling because the solar plexus — the centre of the emotions on the soul plane — is affected.

If she answers to the name of Nic, the chart will look different, but still gives her that valuable 5 and the 3.

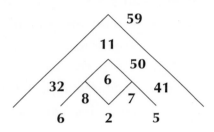

During the time leading up to her first pyramid at age 32, Nicole had already had acting roles in several films (in 1987, at the age of 20, she won her first Australian Film Award). Since then she has starred in many films, giving her the chance to be a VIP on that first peak, which is an 8. In 1990 she met and married Tom Cruise and became even more widely known during this relationship. She and Tom divorced in 2001 when Nicole was 34 years old. So leading up to and during that first peak 8 on her pyramids, despite the divorce, life for Nicole was eventful and largely successful.

On her second peak, a 7, Nicole will continue to reap acclaim and rewards for her work in films, but she will also experience personal hurts and sacrifices. She may widen her thinking and involvement with regard to global issues.

Nicole is now between her second and third pinnacle (at age 41 to 50,) bringing family matters as well as work-related matters to the fore. Let's hope she's in good health because the fourth pinnacle under the 11, at the age of 59 and for the rest of her life, she will have many varied experiences including deepening feelings and actions for humanitarianism on a global scale.

We hope to see her in more films in the future

STEVE IRWIN, CROCODILE HUNTER, ENVIRONMENTALIST

BIRTHDATE: 22/2/1962

Died: 4/9/2006.

Birthdate

Ruling number is 6 (mental plane: love of home, family and all of creation).

Day number is 22/4 (strong number on the soul plane; intuitive).

Arrow of scepticism and orthodoxy (no 3, 5, 7) (traditional / conventional).

One 1 on physical plane (difficulty talking about things other than family and animals).

Four 2s (expresses emotions very openly).

PYN in 2006 was 5.

Watching Steve with his beloved animals and listening to him talk about them, we would be forgiven if we believed that he was a 'gung-ho' person and a little 'over the top' in everything he did and said. He was certainly passionate about the things he loved. But Steve only had two loves — the love for his family and love for the animal kingdom. He was absorbed in these worlds. Outside of these, he was uncomfortable. Steve was a shy, non-egotistical individual, but happy and hugely expressive (the four 2s), ready and more than willing to talk about his loves. Steve lived his life enthusiastically in his conventional, traditional worlds (arrow of orthodoxy).

Denied by no one was his flair for dramatics (another characteristic resulting from four 2s on his chart). As a small child, he watched and mimicked his father and learned very early in life to love and handle God's creatures. He was a classic example of ruling number 6 living positively, as he showed his love for all living things and was a man who loved his own home and family. In any other situation, Steve was a bit lost.

A great amount of Steve's inner strength, abilities and determination flowed from his very strong day number of 22/4. Everything he said and did was done in a larger-than-life and positive way. He was someone determined to leave his mark on this earth.

In summary: Steve's birthdate chart shows the responsibility (6 and 9 together) he felt for what he would call 'his family' (his wife, children and all the animals). The four 2s gave him a flair for dramatics and over-emphasising. His 22/4 day number gave him his belief that anything was possible. The absence of 3, 5, 7 gave him his orthodoxy — living his life from an orthodox and traditional platform, keeping to the mould. Added to his shyness was the one 1 on his chart: he was out of his element when asked personal questions.

```
        5        5        9        9
   S  T  E  V  E     I  R  W  I  N
   1  2     4        9  5     5
```

Steve   **Irwin**

The total of the numbers in his name (Steve) emphasised 'danger and daring' through the 8. Among the even numbers, the 8 sits boldly alongside the odd number 5 for danger and daring. Note the two 5s in this chart — among other things, these can stir the emotions; they sit in the centre of the soul plane alongside the four 2s of his birthdate chart.

Note that his last name, Irwin, adds a further two 5s to his combined charts. This name adds to 10 and would have given him his originality, individuality and his daring to be different. The three 9s on the mental plane can incline towards imbalance, impatience and heaviness.

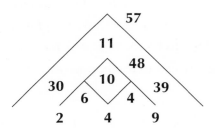

Steve's pyramids expose a 6 on the first peak. Being under a 6 peak influence, especially as a ruling number 6, offers opportunities to be with the public, expand on business and to turn thoughts to family matters. He was under that 6 for nine years before reaching the 4 on his second peak at the age of 39.

Steve at 39, under the influence of 4 on the second peak, continued to build his world and build security for his family. Even though Steve could turn a lemon into lemonade, the 4 can be a difficult influence and in 2005 he was also under the influence of a personal year number 4. In 2006, his personal year number was 5. He would have felt a sense of freedom and ease of movement, especially after the hard work of the previous 4 year compounded by the 4 on the second peak.

His job was often full of danger (at least, by most people's standards) and he had exceptionally dynamic qualities. None of us really knows when and how our life will end. Steve's legacy is inspirational and dynamic, just as he was throughout his life.

NELSON MANDELA, STATESMAN AND PEACE ACTIVIST
BIRTHDATE: 18/7/1918
DIED: 05/12/2013

Birthdate

		9
		88
111		7

Ruling number is 8 (independence, strength of character).
Day number is 9 (love of humanity).
Arrow of frustration (no 4, 5, 6) (loss or loneliness).

Arrow of action (7, 8, 9) (peace-loving; through sacrifice, learns perceptiveness that leads to motivation).
PYN in 2006 was 6.

Nelson Mandela's name is known around the world. His birthdate chart shows separations, loss and disappointments (lack of numbers 4, 5, 6). It also shows motivation and action (numbers 7, 8, 9). The three 1s on his chart gave him the ability to talk and to hold his audience.

His ruling number 8 is a strong masculine number. (Of all the even ruling numbers, 8 joins the odd ruling number 5 in daring action, of which Mr Mandela is the epitome.) He travelled extensively, as indicated by the two 8s on his chart and his ruling number 8. (There are also 8s on the third and fourth peaks of his pyramid. The 8s show restlessness, movement and travel.)

When we examine more thoroughly the arrow of frustration and the arrow of action on Mr Mandela's birthdate chart we get an indication of how he must have felt during his long years of incarceration. Living with the influences of these two arrows would have been like revving a 12-cylinder engine in a car that had its brakes jammed on. He must have felt unbearably frustrated at times.

	5			6			1			5		1
N	E	L	S	O	N	M	A	N	D	E	L	A
5		3	1		5	4		5	4		3	

Nelson

3	6	
	555	
1		

Mandela

3		
	55	
11	44	

While he was imprisoned, the five 5s in his combined name charts would have been causing empty sickness and churning of the stomach — his solar plexus area. But these same 5s would also have helped in his determination to endure and to have a plan once he was freed. The two 4s in his last name kept him down and confined. The 3s from both names gave him hope and his ruling number 8 gave him great strength. Note that the name Nelson, when added, totals 7 and Mandela totals 5. The 7 gave him strength to endure, but it also means sacrifice. The 5 gave the power of steel, but it also means freedom. Interestingly, both names carry the arrow of inactivity.

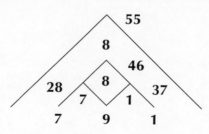

```
              55
               8
                 46
      28    8     37
          7   1
       7     9    1
```

Mr Mandela was called the father of a nation. He was former president of the African National Congress and former president of South Africa. He was imprisoned in the late 1960s and released from prison in 1990. In 1993, along with South Africa's former president, F. W. de Klerk, Mr Mandela accepted the Nobel Peace Prize. His pyramid chart shows his sacrifices and the times when he had to be independent and stand alone (first peak 7, second peak 1, third and fourth peaks 8).

In fact, his pyramid chart exhibits sacrifice and independence all the way. But he rose, exalted. The number 8 played a big part in Mr Mandela's life. His ruling number was 8, he had two 8s on his birthdate chart, his third and fourth pyramid peaks were 8s and at the age of 88, in 2006 (a year totalling 8), he finally retired from such an intense level of public life.

An 8 on a pyramid peak will give the person a chance to be a VIP (in a small or large way). This man earned the respect of billions of people.

DIANA, PRINCESS OF WALES
BIRTHDATE: 1/7/1961
Died: 31/8/1997.

Birthdate

	6	**9**
111		**7**

Ruling number is 7 (lessons learned through sacrifice).

Day number is 1 (able to stand independently).

Arrow of hypersensitivity (no 2, 5, 8) (misunderstandings, touchy).

Numbers 6 and 9 together (responsibility).

Three 1s on chart (good speech-maker; credible).

Isolated 7 on chart (repeated life lessons which can be painful until learned).

PYN in 1997 was 7.

Married in 1981 at the age of 20, divorced in 1996 at the age of 35, Diana was everyone's fairy princess. She looked ethereal and was loved by people around the world. She was graceful and well suited to her positions as princess and patron to various organisations (day number 1 plus three 1s on her chart, as well as 6 and 9 together indicating the capacity to carry responsibility naturally). Princess Diana visited many charitable bodies, including people with HIV/AIDS and leprosy. She did her research well and was not afraid to visit, and shake or hold the hands of some of those infected by disease.

Note that Princess Diana shared the same ruling number 7 as her mother-in-law, Queen Elizabeth II. The number 7 is very strong and, as both these women had leading roles, the opposing vibrations would have been felt throughout the family.

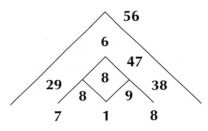

Leading up to her 29th birthday which marked the first peak of her pyramids (an 8), and for nine years beyond, towards her second peak (a 9), she became even more popular around the globe.

She was ambassador for the royal family and England, a benefactor to many, gracious to all she met. She demonstrated a capacity for understanding on many issues.

As a ruling number 7 with the arrow of hypersensitivity, she was strong in many areas but also displayed her soft side and the need, at times, to lean. Diana lived in more than one world. She did her best to assert her strength through her ruling number 7 and her day number of 1. As her soft side emerged, she became ill when she couldn't fight the strength that surrounded her. It seemed that problems, lost love, confusion and in the end, tragedy were all around her.

Looking at her birthdate chart we can see the heavy responsibility Diana had (the 6 and 9 together). The soul plane was empty of numbers (2, 5, 8) making her extremely shy with a tendency towards an inferiority complex. The absence of the 2, 5, 8 will also present with misunderstandings. The isolated 7 on her chart gave her the feeling of being 'cut off'.

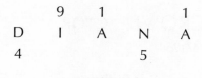

```
        9   1        1
    D   I   A    N   A
    4            5
```

Diana

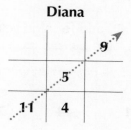

Diana's name number is 2, which is a gentle number, and gave her the power to mix with people and to display her compassion. Her intuition (her ruling number 7 and her name number 2) would have told her many things. She would also undoubtedly have felt humiliated, saying things within the family that would misrepresent her and lead to misunderstandings. The arrow of determination gave her the strength to carry on.

Her pyramid chart shows that at the age of 29 her independence (the 8 on that first peak) made its stand as she travelled the world and cemented the bond between those who loved and respected her as a serious woman seeking to help make the world a better place. Diana died about 18 months before reaching her second peak, a 9, which was leading to universal love and the ending of many things.

RUSSELL CROWE, ACTOR
BIRTHDATE: 7/4/1964

Birthdate

	6	9
1	44	7

Ruling number is 4 (hard worker and good provider).
Day number is 7 (learning through sacrifice).
Arrow of hypersensitivity (no 2, 5, 8) (touchy).

Arrow of practicality (1 ,4, 7) (ideas expressed through the physical).

One 1 on the physical plane (difficulty with personal explanation).

Two 4s on the physical plane (hard, driven worker).

PYN in 2006 was 10.

With a ruling number of 4, a day number of 7 and two 4s on his birthdate chart, Russell has a compounding of heaviness on the physical plane. This provides a strong side to his nature, and as his physical plane is filled (1, 4, 7) everything he does, is done through the physical.

Because of this, at first glance at the chart, it might be thought he is insensitive. This is not so. Russell Crowe has a very sensitive side. His day number of 7 and the absence of 2 ,5, 8 on the soul plane give him great sensitivity. However, with his weighty earth plane, he does have the ability to be physically and verbally hurtful when insensitive people ask sensitive questions of him. Having no numbers on the emotional plane to protect that sensitive nature means that he can be quite touchy.

Having only one 1 on his chart does not help when he really needs to explain himself. (Actors work from a script, so those words come easily.)

Under certain circumstances and because he cannot always say exactly what he would like to say, his frustrations rise and words fail him, so he is likely to say something

really hurtful. Or it may be easier for him simply to pick
up some object and throw it.

In the year 2006, Russell was under the influence of a
personal year number 10. There would have been a few
changes for him under that number and he would also have
made his presence felt. In 2007 his personal year number
is 2. Things may slow down a little for Russell during this
time, but always with some plan going on in the background.

	3			5				3		
R	U	S	S	E	L	L	R	U	S	S
9		1	1		3	3	9		1	1

Russell   **Russ**

333		9		3		9
	5			·······························➤		
11				11		

When the numbers of his first name Russell are added
together they total 7, putting yet another number on that
physical plane. If he were to be called Russ, which may
well be the case in private life, the name numbers add to
5. This would be of some help as the number 5 is on the
emotional plane and adds strength to counteract his real
sensitivity. The 'e' in Russell does the same thing. Either
name also gives two more 1s on the physical plane, giving

him three 1s altogether, which would support his ability to speak in public.

Russell's sensitivity flows through into his films, for example, in his portrayal as John Nash, the brilliant mathematician in the film *A Beautiful Mind*; or as the Roman general, Maximus, in *Gladiator*. Furthermore, his love and sensitivity shone at the birth of his sons.

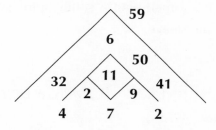

Turning now to Russell's pyramids, we see that at age 32 he came to his first peak, a 2. During this time and the years leading up to the second peak, his life experiences were about handling relationships, learning co-operation and recognising that there was more than one pathway open to him in his life.

Russell reached his second peak, a 9, at age 41. This 9 peak can be a difficult time if he does not apply what he has learned about universal love, understanding, forgiveness and charitable good works, and there may well be emotional experiences. The influence of the 9 on this peak requires him to forget the self and think of others. If he is able to rise to this challenge, his humanitarian and philanthropic aspects will come to the fore. During this period, he might also be affected by changes brought about (perhaps) by someone else.

Russell is now on his third pinnacle – an 11. It would be advantageous for him at this age to have learnt enough about the philosophies of life to keep a balanced outlook while influenced by this number, since life could present him with various challenges. We haven't seen the last of Russ; he's a strong man with a strong spirit and still has a few ideas up his sleeve.

CATHY FREEMAN, OLYMPIC RUNNER
BIRTHDATE: 16/2/1973

Birthdate

Ruling number is 11 (spiritual, intuitive).
Day number is 7 (teacher; sacrifice; selective).
Arrow of the intellect (3, 6, 9) (mental activity, balance).
Arrow of the planner (1, 2, 3) (love of order and planning)
Isolated 7 on chart (repeated learning experiences).
PYN in 2006 was 8.

Cathy is a headstrong woman (mind plane filled). If she were to follow her intuition (2 on the chart and ruling number 11) more often it would make her life just that much easier. There is always someone around Cathy making demands on her time and energy (some are genuine) and being a spiritual person (ruling number 11), she does her best where she can (6 and 9 together on the chart give her a sense of responsibility, and the arrow of the planner means she has good organisational skills). Because of that isolated 7 on her chart, the same experiences of life will continue to plague her until they are recognised and dealt with.

	1			
C	A	T	H	Y
3		2	8	7

Cathy

3		
2		8
1		7

The numbers in Cathy's name total 3, adding to her personality the lightness that millions have come to love. The lack of 4, 5, 6 on the will plane contribute to her tendency to be hesitant at times although this is diluted by the 6 on her birthdate chart.

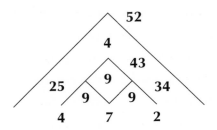

With 9s on the first three peaks of her pyramid chart, Cathy's focus until she is well into her 40s will be humanitarian issues. These 9s also show her capacity for loving all beings, which must be demonstrated during this time. These number 9 influences might also urge her to travel, while at the same time she will want to stay at home to do what she can for others there as well. With each passing year, Cathy will learn to handle the challenges she faces and will continue with her charity work.

Cathy was under the vibration of a PYN 8 in 2006 and she would have felt her independence. A PYN 8 is a year of growth and prosperity, and with wisdom, she can take advantage of the new opportunities it has offered.

Cathy might be hoping that life will have some changes for her. She's most likely been feeling the heaviness of the past 18 years.

But life is what it is and as the years go by it's expected that we learn how to make it easier as we approach the next focal point on our pathway.

Cathy is a lovely soul and even as the years go by this will still shine from her. She'll continue on for the next several years as she has done in the past, since the age of 25. When Cathy reaches 52, a big change will arrive in the way her life presents.

She's been under the personal year number 8 in 2015, making her restless, but in 2016 when her personal year number becomes 9, there will be changes.

IAN THORPE, OLYMPIC SWIMMER
BIRTHDATE: 13/10/1982

Birthdate

3		9
2		8
1 1		

Ruling number 7 (philosopher, sacrifice, reserved).
Day number 4 (good friend, dependable, hard worker).
Arrow of frustration (no 4, 5, 6) (can be hesitant).
Arrow of the planner (1, 2, 3) (love of order, likes to plan).
Three 1s (bright and interesting; good at public speaking).
PYN in 2006 was 4.

Ian has tremendous support from his strong ruling number 7 and his day number 4. Ruling number 7, though, often sets people a little apart, so that they feel different from the rest. In his speech announcing his retirement from competitive swimming late in 2006, Ian expressed a desire to catch up on those things he had so far neglected in his life: in a sense, fulfil his yearning to lead a more 'normal' lifestyle.

His day number 4 offers some clues to the setbacks he experienced during 2006, along with the fact that for him this was a PYN 4. Another challenge for Ian is the empty arrow down the centre of his chart — the absence of 4, 5, 6 — the arrow of frustration. This does not mean that Ian has no will power. But it does present as a reluctance or hesitancy at times to enact his plans (he also has the arrow of the planner).

9	1				6			9	5
I	A	N		T	H	O	R	P	I	E
		5		2	8		9	7		

Ian   Thorpie

Whether Ian is called 'Ian' or 'Thorpie' his name adds strength to his birthdate chart. Both names offer him a 5 on the chart, assisting him with emotional balance. This is strongest in 'Thorpie' which has the soul / emotional plane (2, 5, 8) completely filled. On the other hand, 'Ian' offers him the arrow of determination (1, 5, 9).

2007 is a PYN 5 for Ian during which he will experience a wonderful feeling of freedom. He is likely to explore various new opportunities and to express himself more fully.

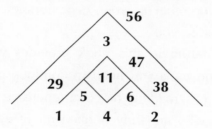

At 24, Ian is still some years away from the first peak on his pyramids.

Ian has moved on smoothly since his interview with Sir Michael Parkinson in 2014 where he told Michael and the world that he is a gay man.

Thorpie has now retired from professional swimming after his shoulder injury, especially when he discovered it was more serious than first thought.

According to the second pinnacle on his pyramids – a 6 – It looks as though he could participate in a business venture, which will be profitable. Will it be Media?

Television? Thorpie currently devotes his time to his Fountain for Youth Foundation and the charity Life Line.

IN CONCLUSION

If you have read this book cover to cover, or even if you have simply dipped into it here and there, no doubt you have felt an irresistible urge — many times — to check out some aspect or other of your own numbers or those of someone close to you.

The information in this book provides you with the knowledge and tools you need to continue practising the drawing up and reading of comprehensive numerology charts. Those who are truly hooked might even go on to attend classes or workshops.

ACKNOWLEDGMENTS

With heartfelt thanks to my brother, Eric Johns, who was ever at my call when I needed help. Special thanks to my sister, Wendy Robb for her advice and encouragement, and to my nephew, Howard Johns and my friend Sandra Burcher for their help when my computer played up. Further thanks to my friends Jan McIntyre, Roslyn Fitzgerald, Jan Saunders and Lucy Disalvo for their moral support.